CUMBRIA LIBRARIES

WAL

LANGDALE

THE LANGDALE FE...

© Mark Richards 2019
Second edition 2019
ISBN: 978 1 78631 032 3

Originally published as Lakeland Fellranger, 2009
ISBN: 978 1 85284 543 8

Printed in China on behalf of Latitude Press Ltd
A catalogue record for this book is available from the British Library.
All photographs are by the author unless otherwise stated.
All artwork is by the author.

Maps are reproduced with permission from HARVEY Maps,
www.harveymaps.co.uk

Updates to this Guide

While every effort is made by our authors to ensure the accuracy of guide-books as they go to print, changes can occur during the lifetime of an edition. Any updates that we know of for this guide will be on the Cicerone website (www.cicerone.co.uk/1032/updates), so please check before planning your trip. We also advise that you check information about such things as transport, accommodation and shops locally. Even rights of way can be altered over time. We are always grateful for information about any discrepancies between a guidebook and the facts on the ground, sent by email to updates@cicerone.co.uk or by post to Cicerone, Juniper House, Murley Moss, Oxenholme Road, Kendal, LA9 7RL.

Register your book: To sign up to receive free updates, special offers and GPX files where available, register your book at www.cicerone.co.uk.

Front cover: Walkers approaching Crinkle Crags backed by Pike o'Blisco

Title page: Pike o'Stickle from above Langdale Combe

CONTENTS

Typical rough ridge trail on Crinkle Crags

Key to route maps and topos

 Route on a defined path

 Route on an intermittent or undefined path

12 **Starting point**

4 **Route number** (on topos)

▲ **Fell summit** featured in this guide (on maps)

 Fell summit featured in this guide (on maps)

3 **Route number** (on maps)

N

0   500
m

1:40,000

Harvey map legend

 Lake, small tarn, pond

River, footbridge

Wide stream

Narrow stream

Peat hags

Marshy ground

Contours change from brown to grey where the ground is predominantly rocky outcrops, small crags and other bare rock.

Improved pasture

Rough pasture

Fell or moorland

Open forest or woodland

Dense forest or woodland

Felled or new plantation

Forest ride or firebreak

Settlement

Boundary, maintained
Boundary, remains

On moorland, walls, ruined walls and fences are shown. For farmland, only the outer boundary wall or fence is shown.

Contour (15m interval)

Index contour (75m interval)

Auxiliary contour

Scree, spoil heap

Boulder field

Scattered rock and boulders

Predominantly rocky ground

Major crag, large boulder

O.S. trig pillar, large cairn

Spot height (from air survey)

Dual carriageway

Main road (fenced)

Minor road (unfenced)

Track or forest road

Footpath or old track

Intermittent path

Long distance path

Powerline, pipeline

Building, ruin or sheepfold, shaft

The representation of a road, track or footpath is no evidence of the existence of a right of way.

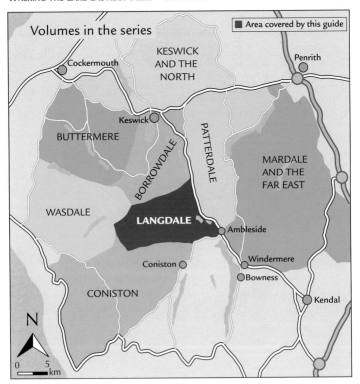

Volumes in the series

■ Area covered by this guide

Cockermouth

KESWICK AND THE NORTH

Penrith

Keswick

BUTTERMERE

BORROWDALE

PATTERDALE

MARDALE AND THE FAR EAST

WASDALE

LANGDALE

Ambleside

Coniston

Windermere

Bowness

CONISTON

Kendal

N

0   5
km

Thirlmere from the north ridge of Steel Fell (photo: Maggie Allan)

Flat Crags on Bowfell

AUTHOR PREFACE

This land of living dreams we call the Lake District is a cherished blessing to know, love and share. As we go about our daily routines, we may take a fleeting moment to reflect that someone, somewhere, will be tramping up a lonely gill or along an airy ridge, peering from a lofty summit or gazing across a wind-blown tarn and taking lingering solace from its timeless beauty. The trappings of modern life thrust carpet and concrete under our feet, and it is always wonderful to walk the region's sheep trods and rough trails, and to imprint our soles upon the fells. This series sets out to give you the impetus and inspiration to make space in your schedule to explore them time and again, in myriad different ways.

However, the regular paths of long tradition deserve our care. Progressively many of the main paths are being re-set with cobbles and pitching by organisations such as Fix the Fells, to whose work you have contributed by buying this guide. But in many instances, the best consideration we can give these pathways is rest. The modern fellwanderer should show a new 'green' awareness by choosing to tread lightly on the land and to find new ways around the hills. One of the underlying impulses of this guide is to protect these beloved fells by presenting a diversity of route options for each and every fell – and also, in this new edition, recommending 'fell-friendly' routes to each summit which are less susceptible to erosion.

Another feature of this latest incarnation of Fellranger, apart from the smaller size to slip in your pocket or pack, is the addition of a selection of inspiring ridge routes at the end of each volume for those of you who like to spend a little longer with your head and feet in the heavenly realms, relishing the summit views and the connections between the felltops, as well as some accompanying online resources for readers with a digital bent.

STARTING POINTS

	Location		GR NY...	Access	Fell ascents described from here
1	Seathwaite	verge parking S of Seathwaite Bridge and before Seathwaite Farm, at the head of Borrowdale	235 123	FP	Esk Pike, Great End, Scafell Pike
2	Stonethwaite	large layby, before the village, at the head of Borrowdale	261 139	FP, B	Bowfell, Esk Pike, High Raise, Rossett Pike, Thunacar Knott
3	Steel End	pay-and-display car park, head of Thirlmere	321 130	PP, B	Calf Crag, High Raise, Steel Fell
4	Dunmail Raise	large layby near summit	329 111	FP, B	Steel Fell
5	Winterseeds	bus stop on A591, 1.5km N of Grasmere	337 088	B	Calf Crag, Gibson Knott, Helm Crag, Steel Fell
6	A591 layby	large layby, 1km N of Grasmere	337 086	FP, B	Blea Rigg, Calf Crag, Gibson Knott, Helm Crag, High Raise, Sergeant Man, Silver How, Tarn Crag
7	Broadgate Meadow	NP car park, Grasmere	338 078	PP, B	Blea Rigg, Calf Crag, Gibson Knott, Helm Crag, High Raise, Sergeant Man, Silver How, Tarn Crag
8	Red Bank Road	council car park, Grasmere	335 073	PP, B	Blea Rigg, Calf Crag, Gibson Knott, Helm Crag, High Raise, Sergeant Man, Silver How, Tarn Crag
9	Stock Lane	NP car park, Grasmere	339 073	PP, B	Blea Rigg, Calf Crag, Gibson Knott, Helm Crag, High Raise, Sergeant Man, Silver How, Tarn Crag
10	White Moss	2 private car parks, either side of the road, by Rydal Water	350 065	PP, B	Loughrigg Fell
11	Pelter Bridge	NP car park, Rydal	365 059	PP, B	Loughrigg Fell
12	Rydal Road	council car park, Ambleside	375 047	PP, B	Loughrigg Fell
13	Clappersgate	large layby on B5286 (and bus stop nearby on the A593)	365 033	FP, B	Loughrigg Fell
14	Tarn Foot	parking at Tarn Foot Farm, by Loughrigg Tarn	345 039	FP	Loughrigg Fell

Location			GR NY...	Access	Fell ascents described from here
15	High Close	NT car park by the youth hostel	337 053	FP	Loughrigg Fell, Silver How
16	Elterwater	NT car park by the river (also free rough parking outside village)	328 048	NT, B	Lingmoor Fell, Silver How
17	Stickle Ghyll	Langdale NP car park and Stickle Ghyll NT car park	295 063	PP, NT, B	Blea Rigg, Bowfell, Harrison Stickle, High Raise, Lingmoor Fell, Loft Crag, Pavey Ark, Sergeant Man, Silver How, Thunacar Knott
18	Old Dungeon Ghyll	NT car park, head of Great Langdale	286 061	NT, B	Bowfell, Crinkle Crags, Esk Pike, Loft Crag, Pike o'Blisco, Pike o'Stickle, Rossett Pike, Scafell Pike
19	Three Shires Inn	verge parking to the E of the inn, Little Langdale	318 034	FP	Lingmoor Fell
20	Blea Tarn	NT car park above Little Langdale	296 043	NT	Lingmoor Fell, Pike o'Blisco
21	Castle Howe	rough parking for a few cars, 0.5km W of Castle Howe, E end of Wrynose Pass	292 032	FP	Pike o'Blisco
22	Wrynose Pass	rough layby parking on both sides of the road at the crest of the pass	277 027	FP	Cold Pike, Crinkle Crags, Pike o'Blisco
23	Wrynose Bottom	rough verge parking on the north side, just past Wrynose Breast, W end of Wrynose Pass	266 023	FP	Cold Pike
24	Cockley Beck Bridge	layby between Wrynose and Hardknott Passes	246 016	FP	Bowfell, Crinkle Crags, Little Stand
25	Brotherilkeld	layby at the foot of Hardknott Pass	210 012	FP	Bowfell, Crinkle Crags, Esk Pike, Scafell Pike
26	Wha House	small car park N of Wha House Farm, head of Eskdale	200 009	FP	Scafell Pike
27	Wasdale Head	NT car park	183 075	NT	Scafell Pike
28	Wasdale Head Village Green	lots of rough parking (but fills up in season)	186 085	FP	Great End, Scafell Pike

FP – free parking

PP – pay parking (NP – National Park)

NT – National Trust (free to members)

B – on a bus route (in season)

Harrison Stickle from above Wall End

INTRODUCTION

Valley bases

Two valleys dominate the area covered by this volume – Great Langdale and the Rydal/Grasmere catchment of the River Rothay. Since the birth of outdoor tourism Ambleside has been pivotal to the Langdale and Grasmere fells, and remains so. It's a rising crescendo of mountain drama to suit all levels of ability and aspiration. From the charming delights of Lingmoor and Loughrigg, which boasts the greatest concentration of paths per square mile of any Lakeland fell, to the majestic circle of summits rising above Mickleden, and beyond to Scafell Pike, these are the realms of serious mountaineering ambition.

Despite the narrow roads there is excellent access and car parking. And once you set forth from your car or bus stop you quickly escape the crowds, finding peace, beauty and worthy challenge on fells that are both steep and craggy. Walks from the Vale of Grasmere to Silver How, Helm Crag and Easedale Tarn draw you into a fabulous arena of wildness that extends higher and higher, culminating on the Langdale Pikes and High Raise. Fellwalkers ultimately cannot resist the wonderful combination of heights at the head of Great Langdale itself: Pike o'Blisco, Crinkle Crags and Bowfell, from where the Scafell massif can be seen in true perspective across the wild head of Eskdale. You can even contemplate climbing Scafell Pike from the Old

↑ *Langdale Pikes from a notch in the summit of Pike o' Blisco (photo: Maggie Allan)* 13

Dungeon Ghyll – a serious mountain day but enormously rewarding, as is all the fellwalking in this corner of Lakeland.

Facilities

The majority of walkers visiting Great and Little Langdale base themselves in Ambleside, a popular holiday destination for well over a century and well supplied with all styles of accommodation. There are also plenty of options in and around Grasmere and Rydal if that is the valley you are exploring. As long as you have a car there are also many hotels, B&Bs and self-catering cottages accessible, as well as hostels and camp sites, scattered all around this area. (The Visit Cumbria website – www.visitcumbria.com, click Accommodation –

The village of Grasmere from Silver How

seems to have the best database or you could just use a search engine.)

Both areas also have grocery shops, cashpoints and a range of places to eat or just savour the local real ales – as well as a high concentration of outlets for browsing the latest range of mountain clothing and gear.

Getting around

Public transport may be a problem elsewhere but in the heart of Lakeland one may confidently plan a day around a reliable rural service, given a proper study of the timetables. For many the first point of arrival is the end of the Lakes Line railway from Kendal at Windermere, right under Wainwright's first-found Lakes viewpoint, Orrest Head. When it comes to buses on from this point, regular Stagecoach services throughout the district are supplemented by the Mountain Goat minibus service. Pertinent to this guide is the 555 Freedom of the Lakes service, which runs along the A591 from Windermere via Ambleside and Grasmere, crossing Dunmail Raise bound for Keswick. This connects, at Ambleside, with the Langdale Rambler service 516 running via Elterwater to the Old Dungeon Ghyll Hotel and the Borrowdale Rambler service 79 from Keswick to Seatoller, giving access to Stonethwaite and Seathwaite. (Check www.traveline.info for train and bus information.)

Parking is not to be taken for granted anywhere in this popular national park. Always allow time to find an alternative parking place, if not to switch to a different plan for your day, unless you are fortunate enough to be able to set out directly from your door, which is perfectly possible if you find accommodation within any of the two valleys. Also take care always to park safely and only in laybys and car parks, not on the side of the narrow country roads. Depending on where you are basing yourself, consider joining the National Trust (www.nationaltrust.org.uk) in order to use their car parks for free. Consult the Starting points table to find out where they, and other parking places, are.

Fix the Fells

The Fellranger series has always highlighted the hugely important work of the Fix the Fells project in repairing the most seriously damaged fell paths. The mighty challenge has been a great learning curve and the more recent work, including complex guttering, is quite superb. It ensures a flat foot-fall where possible, easy to use in ascent and descent, and excess water escapes efficiently minimising future damage.

The original National Trust and National Park Authority partnership came into being in 2001 and expanded with the arrival of Natural England, with additional financial support from the Friends of the Lake District and now the Lake District Foundation (www.lakedistrictfoundation.org). But, and it's a big but, the

Pitched path taking the pressure of pedestrian traffic up Rossett Gill on the way to Rossett Pike

15

whole endeavour needs to raise £500,000 a year to function. This enormous figure is necessary to keep pace with the challenges caused by the joint tyranny of boots and brutal weather. The dedicated and highly skilled team, including volunteers, deserve our sincerest gratitude for making our hill paths secure and sympathetic to their setting. It is a task without end, including pre-emptive repair to stop paths from washing out in the first place.

Mindful that a metre of path costs upwards of £200 there is every good reason to cultivate the involvement of fellwalkers in a cause that must be dear to our hearts… indeed our soles! Please make a beeline for www.fixthefells. co.uk to make a donation, however modest. Your commitment will, to quote John Muir, 'make the mountains glad'.

Using this guide

Unlike other guidebooks which show a single or limited number of routes up the Lakeland fells, the purpose of the Fellranger series has always been to offer the independent fellwalker the full range of approaches and paths available and invite them to combine them to create their own unique experiences. A valuable by-product of this approach has been to spread effects of walkers' footfall more evenly over the path network.

This guide is divided into two parts: 'Fells' describes ascents up each of the 25 fells covered by this volume, arranged in alphabetical order. 'Ridge Routes' describes a small selection of popular routes linking these summits.

Fells

In the first part, each fell chapter begins with an information panel outlining the character of the fell and potential starting points (numbered in blue on the guide overview map and the accompanying 1:40,000 HARVEY fell map, and listed – with grid refs – in Starting Points in the introduction). The panel also suggests neighbouring fells to tackle at the same time, including any classic ridge routes. The 'fell-friendly route' – one which has been reinforced by the National Park or is less vulnerable to erosion – is also identified for those particularly keen to minimise their environmental impact.

After a fuller introduction to the fell, summarising the main approaches and expanding on its unique character and features, come the route descriptions. Paths on the fell are divided into numbered sections. Ascent routes are grouped according to starting point and described as combinations of (the red-numbered) path sections. The opportunities for exploration are endless.

The summit of Steel Fell on the Greenburn Horseshoe (photo: Andrew Leaney)

For each ascent route, the ascent and distance involved are given, along with a walking time that should be achievable in most conditions by a reasonably fit group of walkers keen to soak up the views rather than just tick off the summit. (Over time you will be able to gauge your own likely timings against these figures.) To avoid appearance of impossibly precise accuracy, in the route information distance has been rounded to the nearest 0.1km (and ¼ mile) and ascent/descent to the nearest 5m (and 5ft). Please note that conversions can only therefore be approximate.

In many instances a topo diagram is provided, alongside the main fell map, to help with visualisation and route planning. When features shown on the maps or diagrams appear in the route descriptions for the first time (or the most significant time for navigational purposes), they are highlighted in **bold**, to help you trace the routes as easily as possible.

As a good guide should also be a revelation, panoramas are provided for a small number of key summits and panoramas for every fell in this guide can be downloaded free from www.cicerone.co.uk (see 'Additional online resources' below). These name the principal fells and key features in the direction of view.

Advice is also given at the end of each fell chapter on routes to neighbouring fells and safe lines of descent should the weather close in. In fell-walking, as in any mountain activity, retreat is often the greater part of valour.

Ridge routes

The second part of this guide describes some classic ridge routes in the Langdale area. Beginning with an information panel giving the start and finish points, the summits included and a very brief overview, each ridge route is described step by step, from start to finish, with the summits and other features that appear on the accompanying map highlighted in bold in the text to help you orientate yourself with the HARVEY route map provided. Some final suggestions are included after the main routes for expeditions which you can piece together yourself from the comprehensive route descriptions in 'Fells'.

Appendices

For more information about facilities and services in the Lake District, some useful phone numbers and websites are listed in Appendix A. Appendix B offers a glossary to help newcomers decode the language of the fells as well as some explanations of some of the most intriguing place names that you might come across in this area. Appendix C is a comprehensive list of all the fells included in this 8-volume series to help you decide which volume you need to buy next!

Safety and access

Always take a map and compass with you – make a habit of regularly looking at your map and take pride in learning how to take bearings from it. In mist this will be a time-, and potentially a life-, saver. The map can enhance your day by showing additional landscape features and setting your walk in its wider context. That said, beware of the green dashed lines on Ordnance Survey maps. They are public rights of way but no guarantee of an actual route on the ground. There are many anomalies, such as the bridleway striking up from the dale bottom over the southeast shoulder of Little Stand towards Crinkle Crags which you will struggle to trace on the ground. Take care to study the maps and diagrams provided carefully and plan your route according to your own capabilities and the prevailing conditions.

I beseech you not to rely solely on your mobile phone or other electronic device for navigation. Local mountain rescue teams report that this is increasingly the main factor in the incidents they attend.

Please note that Scafell Pike, although perennially popular and on occasion crowded, is not to be undertaken lightly or in poor weather conditions by any route. The Wasdale Mountain Rescue Team is called to the fell far too often searching for inexperienced, ill-informed, ill-equipped and frequently ill-tempered walkers. Do not, on any account, attempt to connect Scafell with Scafell Pike across Mickledore by Broad Stand. Lord's Rake is also extremely dangerous.

The author has taken care to follow time-honoured routes, and to keep within bounds of access, yet access and rights of way can change and are not guaranteed. Any updates that we know of to the routes in this guide will be made available on the Cicerone website, www.cicerone.co.uk/1032/updates, and we are always grateful for information about discrepancies between a guidebook and the facts on the ground, sent by email to updates@cicerone. co.uk or by post to Cicerone Press, Juniper House, Murley Moss, Oxenholme Road, Kendal, Cumbria, LA9 7RL.

Additional online resources

Summit panoramas for all of the fells in this volume can be downloaded for free from the guide page on Cicerone website (www.cicerone.co.uk/1032). You will also find a ticklist of the summits in the Walking the Lake District Fells series here, should you wish to keep a log of your ascents. For further information about the series, visit www.cicerone.co.uk/fellranger.

The Langdale Pikes from Great Knott

1 BLEA RIGG 556M/1824FT

Climb it from	Stickle Ghyll **17** or Grasmere **6–9**
Character	Highest of a fascinating cluster of craggy tops along a broad ridge
Fell-friendly route	9
Summit grid ref	NY 302 078
Link it with	Silver How or Sergeant Man
Part of	The Easedale Skyline

From the curious knob of Sergeant Man, a long arm of fell draws southeast off the high plateau of High Raise terminating, after some 8km, on Loughrigg Fell, with Blea Rigg and Silver How the only notable summits. From the east, Blea Rigg, in dark silhouette, looks every inch a bastion and, on its northern face, Blea Crag forms a solid buttress commanding attention from Easedale Tarn, Tarn Crag and, surprisingly, from high on Sergeant Man. From other angles its profile is much less distinctive.

Not surprisingly, the best route climbs up from Easedale Beck and Easedale Tarn, from flower meadows to foaming falls, leading walkers by lapping waters and barren fellsides and culminating in the steady pull above Blea Crag. And

↑ *Blea Rigg from the top of Whitegill Crag*

the summit is well worth reaching with majestic views from Helvellyn to the Coniston Fells as well as up close and personal insights on the mighty Langdales.

The shortest climbs lead up from Great Langdale and there are many to choose from, via Stickle Ghyll (Routes 1–3), White Gill (4–5) or Pye Howe (6). Approaches from Grasmere have great charm and scenic variety. You can wander up by Blindtarn Moss to Swinescar Hause (7 and 8), take the classic Easedale Tarn route (9) or sneak up from the northwest via Belles Knott (10).

Ascent from Stickle Ghyll 17

There are three basic lines of approach from this dramatic valley setting. In such surroundings you can be sure of scenic adventure whatever your objective.

Via Stickle Ghyll →*3.2km/2 miles* ↑*475m/1560ft* ⏱*2hr 10min*
1 Walk up the lane past the **New Dungeon Ghyll Hotel**. From the gate head straight on through the small enclosures, and then on beside the tree-shaded beck as it rises to a footbridge. Cross this and then cross a stile to enter the

21

main amphitheatre of this hugely popular ravine. The path, on which much attention has necessarily been lavished over the years, passes up through an old fold and zig-zags via fenced saplings. From this point, by far the majority of walkers choose to keep beside the beck all the way to the tarn. At the top, turn right to follow the path running along the lakeshore. From the edge of the lake a clear, occasionally cairned path leads north, then east, onto the plateau of Blea Rigg.

2 Alternatively, take the path which branches right. This excellent path winds up to run under **Tarn Crag** and reach the outflow of **Stickle Tarn** and turn right with join Route **1**.

3 There is a far more pleasant and less well-known line. Directly after leaving the New Dungeon Ghyll, cross the footbridge located half-right after the initial gate. The path runs behind Millbeck Farm and enters a lane that rises onto the bracken ridge, keeping left to avoid an outcrop. There are two

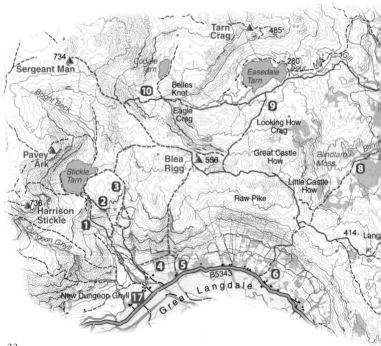

options here. Contour onto the main zig-zagging path, climbing off this as it shapes towards **Tarn Crag**, and wind up to the left of a walled enclosure, or climb, with little initial evidence of a path, in the bracken. On finding a green path skirt the left-hand shoulder of a knoll above an incised gill and traverse the walled enclosure diagonally to join up with the upper section of the old shepherds' path. This then slips over a saddle depression to meet up with the path that runs along the southern shore of the tarn from the outflow. Here, turn right to follow Route **1** to the summit.

Via White Gill →2km/1¼ miles ↑465m/1525ft ⏱2hr

There are two approaches to Whitegill Crag – Route 4, the more direct route up behind the New Dungeon Ghyll Hotel, or Route 5, the climbers' approach to Scout Crag, off the valley road. The latter involves a little mild scrambling.

4 Pass up by the hotel to the bridle-gate, slant right in the triangular enclosure and cross the footbridge. The path rises above Millbeck Farm via a hand-gate with a walled gill gangway. Go through the kissing-gate on the right after 100m, keep the wall to the right and pass through the foot of a larch plantation to cross a low wall into the bouldery ravine of White Gill to join Route **5**.

5 Alternatively, go east along the valley road, passing the entrance to Millbeck Farm, to reach a stile/gate with a National Trust notice below a field-barn. Pass up above the field-barn to a wall-stile, climbing to the left of the lower buttress, a popular training ground for novice climbers. Cross the ladder-stile, ignore the climbers' path rising right to **Scout Crag**, and

23

instead follow the wall immediately left, with little hint of a
path, to enter White Gill. The
combined effects of path and
gill erosion make this a loose,
clambering stretch. Above the
tree trend to the left for bigger boulder steps and more
secure footing. Much of the
gill-bed is dry, with subterranean flow. The view out of
the ravine is superb, leading
the eye across Side Pike to
Wetherlam. The natural exit
draws into a short, tight gully
to the right, requiring a spot
of mild scrambling. Ignore
the gill-head itself. The rock
walls of Whitegill Crag are
hugely impressive and can be
best surveyed by wandering
onto the open spur to the left

Rock pool

once the hard work has been done. The summit of Blea Rigg beckons across
undulating outcrops and slopes. While there is no evident path, a route is
easily concocted. From this approach the perched summit cairn looks like a
bird of prey.

Via Pye How →3.2km/2 miles ↑480m/1575ft ⊕2hr 15min

*A pleasing path, especially allow time for frequent pauses to look back at the
stunning surround of majestic fells.*

6 Follow the road for about a kilometre east from the car parks to reach a
footpath which starts just before **Pye Howe**. A kissing-gate gives entry into a
pasture, the path initially keeping the wall to the left. Ascend following half-a-
dozen waymark posts and cross broken intermediate walls with much mature
scrub colonising the enclosures. A ladder-stile crosses the intake wall at the

top. The path, at first stony, becomes a pleasant turf trail, and, beyond the solitary, gill-shading holly bush, winds steadily to the ridge-top at Swinescar Hause. Joining the ridge path, track left up from the marshy hollow by the old fold and curious cramped shelter.

Traverse **Little Castle How** and **Great Castle How**, passing pools adorned with cotton grass and bogbean. From a cluster of quartz rocks admire a splendid view west to the striking dark profile of Blea Rigg, the obvious culmination of the northward-plunging Blea Crag. The summit is confirmed by the presence of a walled rock shelter directly below. The ridge path waltzes by to the right so that many a head-down fellwalker misses the summit and takes the next prominent cairnless outcrop to the west to be the ultimate point.

Ascent from Grasmere 6–9

Three good paths make use of the Easedale Road (7) to lead up the Easedale valley, towards (8), as far as (9) and beyond (10) the iconic tarn.

Via Blindtarn Moss →*4.5km/2¾ miles* ↑*495m/1625ft* ⏲*2hr 20min*
7 From Sam Read's bookshop in the middle of the village walk north along Easedale Road via Goody Bridge. A few paces short of Oak Lodge, cross the **Easedale Beck** footbridge. A long view of Sour Milk Gill backed by Tarn Crag beckons across flower meadows, the beginning of a fine wild trail. A part-paved path leads past New Bridge, and on reaching a gate (with a yellow waymark) the first route option begins.

8 Go through this gate, entering a meadow, and continue on by open woodland to join the access track at a gate leading to a pair of holiday

LOOKING **SOUTHWEST**

cottages. Glance by these to a gate. Beyond the gate, the path trends up by the beck and leftward to a footpath waymark post that guides right into the hollow of **Blindtarn Moss**. The abundance of bushes ensures plenty of bird-song. The scene is quite unique – a wild Chinese garden in the fells. The path climbs up through the juniper, and higher up, as the ground steepens, the cairned path is worn to loose stones.

Either follow the remnants of the path to the soggy saddle of Swinescar Hause or, just prior to the top, slant onto the right-hand side to follow the old green zig-zag path which offers sweeter footing to rise onto the westward-climbing path above the quaint stone bivvy shelter. Join the ridge path and Route **6** to bear northwest and west to the summit bluff.

Via Easedale Tarn →5km/3 miles ↑490m/1610ft ⏱2hr 30min

9 The popular path to Easedale Tarn leads to the next gate and over the **Blindtarn Gill** bridge, heading straight across the open meadow (ignore the farm track right to Brimmer Head). Go through a gateway and subsequent kissing-gate. The paved path enters a lane which funnels, then opens, wind-ing up above **Sour Milk Gill**. The best view of the falls is from the base of the sheepfold but there is no ready path down. Only the upper fall can be easily reached from the path, and its plunge pool can be the scene of much splash-ing and excited chatter on hot summer afternoons. Thankfully the path has received considerable remedial paving.

Easedale Tarn itself continues to attract walkers, many of whom, as has long been the case, are quite content to make it the ultimate point of their walk, backtracking via the Stythwaite Steps footbridge at the foot of Far Easedale. Either side of the tarn, conical drumlins emphasise the glacial ori-gins of this bleak amphitheatre. The domed top of Tarn Crag looms close right, while Blea Crag forms the southern sidewall, with the sub-edge peak of Belles Knott shielding Codale Tarn a little to its right. Follow the path above the tarn, and watch for a small cairn where the Blea Rigg path very evidently branches left. This winds up above the drumlins seeking the natural dip in the ridge. Either continue to the saddle, close to the perched boulder, or angle up right behind Blea Crag via a rake.

Via Belles Knott →6.5km/4 miles ↑500m/1640ft ⏱2hr 45min

10 As a final option, continue on the south side of **Easedale Tarn**. The path leads up beside the main feeder-gill, with several stepped sections beside the

Ridge cairn above Raw Pike

cascades, and is overlooked by the arresting peak of Belles Knott up to the right, a well-respected scramblers' route and object of photographic composition. Above the falls a side-path bears right, fording the gill, to visit the hanging waters of Codale Tarn, with its tiny outflow and picturesque isle set beneath the great slope of Codale Head. The main path zig-zags up to a ridge-top path interchange, where you turn left, southeast, and wander a kilometre to the summit.

The summit

Several rocky tops vie for pre-eminence here, and conventional mapping offers only slack captioning to add to the confusion. The one sure clue is the presence of a cairn sitting on top of a blade of rock, directly above the shelter passed on the eastern approach. This is the culmination of the outcrop above Blea Crag, and the high point seen from Great Castle How. The view is superb, with Pavey Ark and Harrison Stickle the mighty neighbours. The Helvellyn chain rises invitingly to the east above the serried ridges overlooking Easedale, and the Coniston Fells tantalise beyond Lingmoor Fell and Side Pike.

Pool with bogbean

Safe descents

With crags close to the northern brink, great care is required in poor conditions. The ridge path is plain enough in most situations, but the safest bet is to follow the ridge path running E (**6**). This leads under the summit by the walled shelter, down to the first depression. Bear left (**9**), descending northeastwards through a shallow hollow east of Blea Crag and down to the popular path running close to Easedale Tarn. This path leads by Sour Milk Gill, to the safety of the Easedale meadows (**7**) and into Grasmere.

Ridge routes

Silver How → *3.2km/2 miles* ↓*205m/675ft* ↑*45m/150ft* ⏱ *1hr*
The twists and turns of the ridge trail ensure an entertaining march. En route pass two sizable pools and a cluster of quartz stones by the path, prior to crossing Great Castle How. Deviate left to its top for a dramatic view of Codale Head, while the opposing and seldom-visited Raw Pike gives a fine view over Great Langdale. Beyond Swinescar Hause the ridge is of a more rolling nature, with more pools, the largest consumed by weed. The path runs

under the higher top of Lang How (by nearly 19m) and crosses the head-stream of Wray Gill to reach the scarp-top summit.

Sergeant Man →*2km/1¼ miles* ↓*15m/50ft* ↑*205m/675ft* ⏱*45min*
The occasional cairn indicates a surprisingly modest ridge trail. Immediately after the fourth mock-summit knoll notice where a small section of marsh has been fenced off to evaluate the effects of non-grazing. Just short of the path interchange admire the rock basin formed by Harrison Stickle and Pavey Ark. Cairns now abound. From here the ridge narrows, with rocky outcrops, including one notable tilted slab. The path forks, then the two halves reunite, on the steady climb to the outflow of the marsh west of Codale Head. The summit is swiftly attained on the well-worn final stretch.

Blea Rigg from Redacre Gill

2 BOWFELL 903M/2963FT

Climb it from	Old Dungeon Ghyll **18**, Cockley Beck Bridge **24**, Brotherilkeld **25** and Stonethwaite **2**
Character	An elegant fell shielded by crags, a commanding viewpoint
Fell-friendly route	1
Summit grid ref	NY 245 065
Link it with	Crinkle Crags or Esk Pike
Part of	The Great Langdale Round

Appealing as the Langdale Pikes may be, they are like courtiers in the wings, deferring to the real overlord of Great Langdale. With the rough skyline of Crinkle Crags the heads of high officials, and lowly Rossett Pike the court jester, you just know where the centre of power lies. Missing the magical 3000ft by a mere 37, Bowfell does clear the alternative mountain-threshold of 900m convincingly. But it's not the measurements that make this peak a mountain. Bowfell looms large whether viewed from Eskdale, Langstrath or Great Langdale – but it is most admired, and climbed, from the latter.

    The fell has two craggy aspects: the southern gullied wall of Bowfell Links and the sterner, upper eastern facade of crags, dominated by Bowfell Buttress, a famous proving ground for climbers, and the giant tilted slab-top of Flat Crags,

↑ *Bowfell from Crinkle Crags*

delight of the more adventurous fellwalker, although access to its base can be tricky in poor weather. Just to the north, Angle Tarn has a perennial appeal for high-level campers.

Five contrasting routes (1–5) lead up naturally from the head of Great Langdale. Bowfell's southern approaches from Upper Eskdale (6–7) are wild and remote and require a trekking mindset. The routes up from Borrowdale (8–9) are longer still but follow clear and popular paths.

Ascent from Old Dungeon Ghyll 18

Via the Band →*5.2km/3¼ miles* ↑*810m/2660ft* ⏱*3hr 10min*

No fell-walk more typifies the 'gently, gently, catch your mountain' feeling than the Band, the east ridge approach via Stool End. Climb the spur ridge in nice, easy stages with ample opportunity to admire the neighbouring crags and pikes.

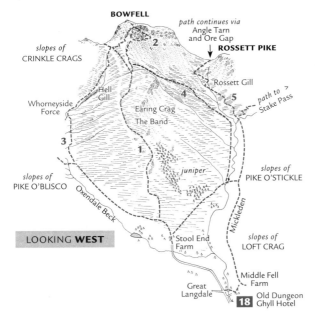

1 Follow the approach road to **Stool End Farm**. Pass through the busy farmyard and, rising from the gate, take the

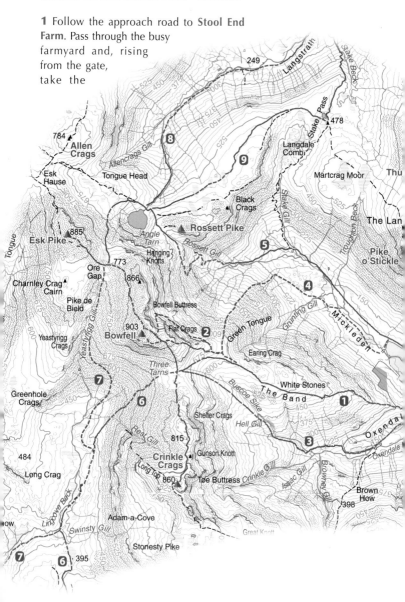

path going right at the brow top. This leads up to a kissing-gate beside the Hamer memorial seat. This popular path has been extensively repaired and is bedecked with an over-abundance of casual cairns. Largely holding to a southern bias, at one point the path momentarily peers over Mickleden to admire Pike o'Stickle and Gimmer Crag, with extensive juniper thicket below. It then takes a side swipe, missing the top of **the Band**. Consider a detour to the brink of **Earing Crag** to look down upon Mickleden. From the subsequent shallow depression (NY 255 062) the path forks. Take the left-hand fork to complete a stony ascent to **Three Tarns** hause (NY 248 061) – it's rare to find more than two pools here. The ridges and gullies that make up Bowfell Links (on the southern face) are well viewed from this point, as too, across the south ridge of Esk Pike, the twin peaks of Scafell and Scafell Pike either side of Mickledore. The right-hand path from the hause takes a rough, stony clambering line up the southern flank of Bowfell, reaching the summit by the top of **Flat Crags**.

Via the Climbers' Traverse and the Great Slab → *5.5km/3¼ miles* ↑*820m/2690ft* ⏲*3hr 30min*

The confident walker, with a head for heights and seasoned mountain feet, may wish to consider following the Climbers' Traverse.

2 Alternatively, take the right-hand fork on the rise up from the depression above **Earing Crag** which rises with the ridge, passing over to the shadowy northern side. It is consistent but narrow. In some respects it is more exposed than Jack's Rake, so in wet, windy or icy conditions most walkers should leave it well alone! The traverse keeps under the banded cliff-end of **Flat Crags** and, from a minor col, gains a handsome view of Bowfell Buttress, flanked by runs

The Climbers' Traverse (photo: Brian Gotts)

of scree, across the combe. Coming under the broken wall of Cambridge Crag, the path switches up left, onto the bouldery corner, running up the tilted slabs of Flat Crags, known as the Great Slab. If the rock is dry you might find it more comfortable, and certainly more entertaining, to walk up the open slab itself – just watch your footing on any wet algae. The topmost outcrop exhibits the banded nature of the bedrock well. Turn left at the top to reach the path from **Three Tarns (1)** and turn right for the summit.

Via Oxendale and Hell Gill → 5.2km/3¼ miles
↑790m/2590ft ⏱3hr 20min

A pleasing variant up to the Three Tarns hause leads by Oxendale to Whorneyside Force and Hell Gill. This route is often used as an alternative descent to the Band, and has been saved from further erosion by exemplary pitching on the steep section at the foot of Hell Gill.

3 The route leads into **Oxendale** from **Stool End Farm**. Ignore the first footbridge. Either keep to the riverbank path, which from the wall-end becomes narrow, or rise right to contour easily on a good path to the second footbridge. The pitched path now curves up the bank. Close to the mare's-tail falls there is land slippage to be wary of. The waterfall and small pool with a large boulder at the top of **Whorneyside Force** give reason to idle. The path next fords the beck via boulders, passes under the embowered entrance to **Hell**

Gill and mounts the path. Take a look into Hell Gill as the slope eases and, higher, admire the composition formed by Pike o'Blisco. The path pays little heed to **Buscoe Sike**, preferring to slant up the damp slope and latterly rising steeply to join the Band path (**1**) just below **Three Tarns**.

Via Mickleden and Green Tongue →5.3km/3¼ miles ↑810m/2660ft ⏱3hr 40min

This is a tough grass route, for which you might need walking poles if you choose to descend it.

4 Follow the valley bridleway from the Old Dungeon Ghyll. At first a lane, it opens out beyond a sheep holding-pen. The wall on the left ends. Bear left, to cross the footbridge spanning **Mickleden Beck**. Go right, along the flat damp dale floor to join a shepherding drove-cum-quad bike trail, consolidated where it fords minor gills draining the Band. Shortly after passing an old fold, tucked down in a bracken-filled hollow, the drove slips right. Keep all the moraine to the right, contouring over damp ground, thus avoiding the bracken, until a rowan tree is spotted in a gill up to the left. Ascend the rigg beside the gill. Continue the steady, breathless climb, the compensation being the fine views of Rossett Gill and, as you gain height, the craggy east face of Bowfell, a famous climbing ground. Higher still venture to the eastern edge to see Earing Crag on the north slope of the Band. Reach the top of **Green Tongue** above the shallow depression where the Band merges with Bowfell proper. Be warned: ignore the first path encountered leading off to the right – this leads to the Climbers' Traverse. Proceed further, slightly descending to hairpin back to join the main path to **Three Tarns** (**1**) and the popular path to the top.

Rossett Gill trail via Angle Tarn and Ore Gap →7km/4¼ miles ↑875m/2870ft ⏱3hr 50min

A circuitous, rocky mountain route to the summit.

5 Follow the valley path up Mickleden. From the footbridge at the foot of **Stake Gill** follow the old pony path left, initially with **Rossett Gill** left. As it becomes excessively stony the path fords the gill. (The old short-cut up the gill is a lost cause. Give it a miss!) The pitched trail veers away leftward, zig-zagging twice to get past the rock outcropping, the second time the more extravagantly. Cresting the top of Rossett Gill, it declines sedately to the outflow of **Angle Tarn**. On the rise beyond take the left-hand fork in the path, which curves from west to south negotiating intermittent bouldery patches to gain the plain saddle at **Ore Gap**. Go left, with plenty of ankle-twisting boulders to test your sense of balance, as the path trends slightly east of south onto the ridge. Short of the final knoll go to the brink and look down the scree gully, with Bowfell Buttress down to the left. Just think, some folk (including your author) have come up this way!

Ascent from Cockley Beck Bridge 24 *off map S* and Brotherilkeld 25 *off map SW*

The River Esk has two principal headstreams which meet in dramatic circumstances at picturesque Lingcove Bridge. Lingcove Beck has two prime points of issue, Ore Gap and Three Tarns, the hauses that define Bowfell to north and south, giving fellwalkers objectives on either route. The swifter but duller approach (6) tracks up Mosedale. The more impressive one (7) begins from Brotherilkeld accompanying the Esk to Lingcove Bridge.

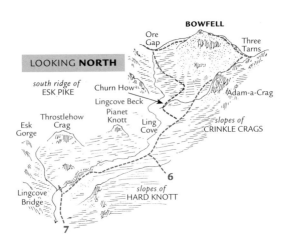

The Scafells from Three Tarns

From Cockley Beck Bridge →6.4km/4 miles ↑825m/2710ft ⏱4hr 15min
6 The bridleway, signposted off the open road west of Cockley Beck Bridge, squelches for 2.5km to the ridge across the dale head. When you reach **Lingcove Beck** turn right to follow it upstream. Passing well below the impressive **Adam-a-Cove**, western buttress of Long Top, slashed by a sinister gully, the path slants northeast up the moraine, then fords **Rest Gill**. There is modest evidence of a path on the steady climb to the two tarns at **Three Tarns**. Turn left with Route **1** to reach the summit from the southeast.

From Brotherilkeld →7.6km/4¾ miles ↑1040m/3410ft ⏱4hr 30min
7 The path trends up right from Brotherilkeld at Lingcove Bridge and forks right to climb above **Lingcove Beck** into Ling Cove. The route from here to Ore Gap is less than obvious. There is little hint of a consistent path contouring round **Churn How**, then ascending a rigg beneath the headwall of Bowfell, well to the right of **Yeastyrigg Gill**. Slanting up left to a prominent skyline boulder, a path now materialises underfoot, coming closer to the gill on the lead into to the pass. From **Ore Gap** go right towards the summit, with Route **5**, on intermittently stony terrain.

Ascent from Stonethwaite 2 *off map N*

Stonethwaite may seem a remote launch pad. However, as Bowfell does have a toe-hold in Borrowdale, many fellwalkers reasonably contemplate including the summit in a through trek to Great Langdale and Cumbria Way hikers can elevate their expedition immeasurably by including it.

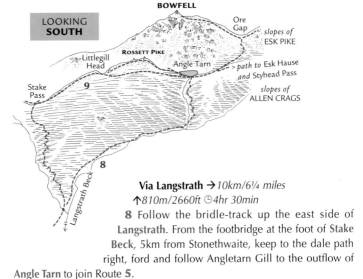

Via Langstrath → *10km/6¼ miles*
↑*810m/2660ft* ⏱*4hr 30min*

8 Follow the bridle-track up the east side of Langstrath. From the footbridge at the foot of **Stake Beck**, 5km from Stonethwaite, keep to the dale path right, ford and follow Angletarn Gill to the outflow of **Angle Tarn** to join Route **5**.

9 Alternatively, reach Angle Tarn by following the Cumbria Way to the top of **Stake Pass** and then taking the ridge path right, with the option to include the summit of **Rossett Pike**. Here join Route **5** to round the tarn to the west and head south to the summit.

The summit

This summit is stone pure and simple – a mix of boulders and bedrock and a place of repose. Catch your breath and take in the marvellous all-round view. No visit is complete without looking over the eastern brink. Descend northeast to meet the path traversing from Ore Gap to Three Tarns or wander

Looking west to the Scafells from the summit

cautiously to the edge of Cambridge Crag for the most sensational view of the Great Slab of Flat Crags and Bowfell Buttress. The view at the brink of Bowfell Links due south is also worth the wander.

Safe descents

With so much craggy ground beneath the summit, finding and keeping to an evident path is crucial. The path running diagonally just E of the summit pile should be used, NNW for Ore Gap (**5**) and SE for Three Tarns (**1**).

Ridge routes

Crinkle Crags →*2.2km/1½ miles* ↓*195m/640ft* ↑*140m/460ft* ⏱*1hr*
A walk to sing about. Head E, joining the main ridge path leading by banded rocks close to the top of the Great Slab of Flat Crags. Leave the plateau SE on an often loose trail to Three Tarns, weave due S, visiting, or circumventing, successive craggy knotts. After Shelter Crags, Gunson Knott is the first true crinkle. The fourth crinkle is the summit.

Esk Pike →*1.6km/1 mile* ↓*120m/395ft* ↑*110m/360ft* ⏱*35min*
Head NNW to Ore Gap, then rise NW straight to the summit.

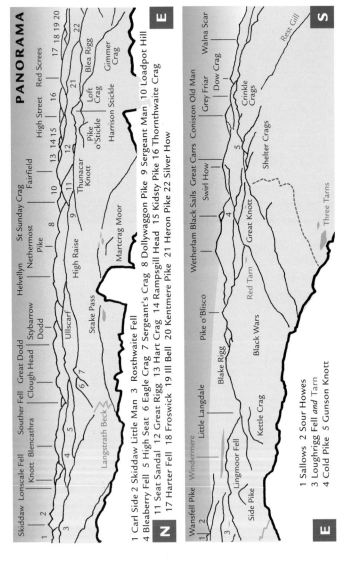

PANORAMA

E

Red Screees High Street Fairfield St Sunday Crag Helvellyn Nethermost Pike Great Dodd Stybarrow Dodd Clough Head Great Dodd Souther Fell Lonscale Fell Skiddaw

17 18 19 20 22 Blea Rigg Loft Crag Gimmer Crag Pike o'Stickle Harrison Stickle Thunacar Knott High Raise Ullscarf Martcrag Moor Stake Pass Langstrath Beck Blencathra Knott

16 21 1415 12 10 13 11 9 8 6 7 5 4 3 2 1

N

1 Carl Side 2 Skiddaw Little Man 3 Rosthwaite Fell
4 Bleaberry Fell 5 High Seat 6 Eagle Crag 7 Sergeant's Crag 8 Dollywaggon Pike 9 Sergeant Man 10 Loadpot Hill
11 Seat Sandal 12 Great Rigg 13 Hart Crag 14 Rampsgill Head 15 Kidsty Pike 16 Thornthwaite Crag
17 Harter Fell 18 Froswick 19 Ill Bell 20 Kentmere Pike 21 Heron Pike 22 Silver How

S

Walna Scar Dow Crag Coniston Old Man Grey Friar Great Carrs Black Sails Wetherlam Swirl How

Rest Gill Crinkle Crags Shelter Crags Great Knott Three Tarns Red Tarn Pike o'Blisco Blake Rigg Black Wars Little Langdale Kettle Crag Lingmoor Fell Side Pike Wansfell Pike Windermere

5 4

E

1 Sallows 2 Sour Howes
3 Loughrigg Fell *and* Tarn
4 Cold Pike 5 Gunson Knott

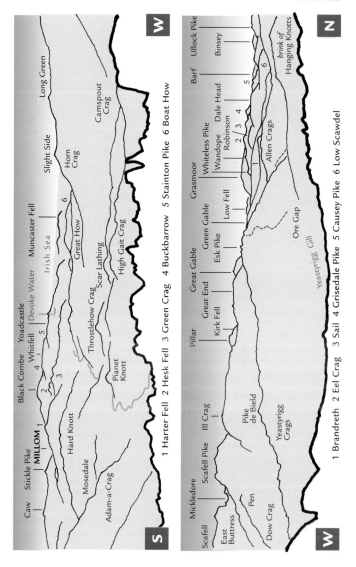

W

N

Long Green — Slight Side — Muncaster Fell — Yoadcastle — Black Combe — Stickle Pike — Caw

Camspout Crag — Horn Crag — Great How — Throstlehow Crag — Scar Lathing — High Gait Crag — Pianet Knott — Hard Knott — Mosedale — Adam-a-Crag

Irish Sea — Devoke Water — Whitfell — MILLOM

S

1 Harter Fell 2 Hesk Fell 3 Green Crag 4 Buckbarrow 5 Stainton Pike 6 Boat How

Ullock Pike — Barf — Grasmoor — Great Gable — Pillar — Mickledore — Scafell

Binsey — brink of Hanging Knotts — Whiteless Pike — Dale Head — Robinson — Wandope — Allen Crags — Low Fell — Esk Pike — Green Gable — Great End — Kirk Fell — Scafell Pike — Ill Crag — Pike de Bield — Yeastyrigg Crags — Pen — Dow Crag — East Buttress

Ore Gap — Yeastyrigg Gill

W

1 Brandreth 2 Eel Crag 3 Sail 4 Grisedale Pike 5 Causey Pike 6 Low Scawdel

41

3 CALF CRAG 537M/1762FT

Climb it from	Mill Bridge **5**, Grasmere **6–9** or Steel End **3**
Character	A modest triangle of high ground presiding over the Wythburn, Greenburn and Far Easedale valleys
Fell-friendly route	2
Summit grid ref	NY 301 104
Link it with	Gibson Knott, Sergeant Man or Steel Fell
Part of	The Greenburn Horseshoe

A curved ridge sweeps northwestward from the of Vale of Grasmere. It begins with Helm Crag, probably Grasmere's best-known and best-loved hill, from where it takes a roller-coaster ride over Gibson Knott, climbing over Pike of Carrs to finish eventually upon Calf Crag. This pivotal but often overlooked point on the Greenburn Horseshoe is best viewed from beneath Deer Bield Crag where its steep southern slopes spill into the wild depths of Far Easedale. To the north, the fell merges soggily into the morass of upper Wythburn Dale.

Calf Crag's considerable distance from valley affairs lends the fell-top a certain lonely mystique. If you make it the summit of your aspirations, rather than using one of the many bypassing routes to speed on in the pursuit of one or other horseshoe route, you may find you have it all to yourself.

↑ *Calf Crag summit looking towards Tarn Crag*

Route 1 tracks its way up through quiet Greenburn Dale from the east, Route 2 follows the southern aspect of Far Easedale from Grasmere, while Route 3 climbs gently up from Wyth Burn to the north.

Ascent from Mill Bridge 5

Via Greenburn Dale →*3.5km/2¼ miles* ↑*440m/1445ft* ⊕*2hr*

Greenburn Dale is a beautiful and less frequented valley, well rewarding a visit for its own sake.

1 Follow the minor road down to the bridge where **Raise Beck** becomes the **River Rothay**. Go right, passing Ghyll Foot. Turn up the drive leading over cattle grids by Helmside and rise to Turn Howe and the subsequent gate onto the fell. Go forward with the green track, leading alongside a wall on the right, then go through a gate into a short lane. This emerges beyond the attractive waterfalls to continue as an unfettered track. Passing moraine, the track bears left and crosses stepping-stones, then goes right to contour past a tidy sheepfold set between boulders. Watch for a cairn marking the point where the path climbs left, up a wet patch, and zig-zags to the saddle. Spot the cairn on the right, which guides onto the clear path climbing **Pike of Carrs**. Sections of eroded peat intervene en route to the summit.

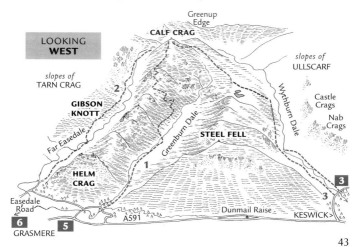

Ascent from Grasmere 6–9

A straightforward route from the centre of the village on clear paths.

Via Far Easedale →5.7km/3½ miles ↑455m/1495ft ⏱2hr 45min

2 Leave Broadgate opposite Sam Read's bookshop, along Easedale Road. This leads naturally onto the signposted bridle-path running into **Far Easedale**. After crossing Stythwaite Steps footbridge keep right, with the one clear path. There are a few rough sections en route to the saddle at the dale head. The metal stakes are all that remain of an old step-stile. Bear acutely right, bound for the summit outcrop which is already in sight beyond the tarn in Brownrigg Moss.

Ascent from Steel End 3

The most remote of the three options makes its way up from the north, with pathless sections but easy gradients.

Via Wythburn Dale →5.5km/3½ miles ↑380m/1245ft ⏱2hr 30min

3 Footpaths lead from either side of the road bridge spanning **Wyth Burn**, opposite the Steel End car park. A further path follows a farm track via a lane stemming off the bridle-way above West Head (formerly known as Steel End before the farmholdings were amalgamated). Negotiate the sequence of ladder-stiles by any of the paths that converge and reach the foot-bridge beneath Rake Crags, just where the valley begins to constrict. Follow the clear path climbing up the south side of the ravine below Black Crag. When the wind blows up the valley the fuming falls can be most impressive, with the spray flying high. The dale opens, becoming progressively more desolate, and, further ahead, the beck slothfully winds through a gently curving tarn. Leave the obvious path as soon as the dale opens out, climb the easy

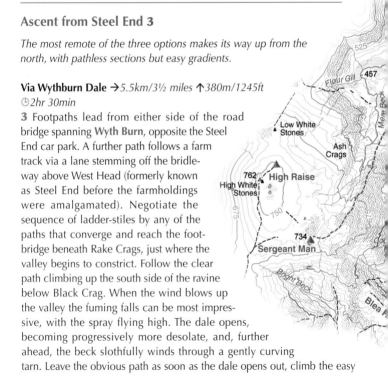

Steel End

516 · Nab Crags

Castle Crags

Wyth Burn

Dunmail Raise

The Bog

468

Steel Fell

Blakerigg Crag

306

Rough Crag

Green Burn

537 · Calf Crag

Pike of Carrs

Gibson Knott

Far Easedale Gill

Horn Crag

355

Helm Crag

The Lion and the Lamb

Deer Bield Crag

Tarn Crag

485

280 Sour Milk Gill

Easedale Tarn

Belles Knot

Eagle Crag

Looking How Crag

Great Castle How

224

Blindtarn Moss

Little Castle How

556

Town Head

Raise Beck

A591

Tonguegill Force

105

Mill Bridge

River Rothay

90

Easedale Beck

Grasmere

slopes (no path) and skirt to the west of the tarns in the wide, shallow depression of the ridge. Join the ridge path from Steel Fell and head damply south to the summit.

The summit

A cairn rests atop a pronounced up-thrusting outcrop. The steep rock face on the Easedale side is high enough to require care in poor visibility. Being hemmed in by the bulky mass of High Raise and Ullscarf ensures that the best elements of a disappointing view are eastward – to the long western wall of Helvellyn and Fairfield. The craggy facade of Tarn Crag, notably Deer Bield Crag, which can be seen across Far Easedale, merits prime attention. Where summits are not much prized, walkers often create 'avoiding paths' around them from existing sheep trods. One such path runs below the summit on the southern flank.

Safe descents

The ridge path E is reliable, if followed meticulously. However, in very poor conditions it may be prudent to head initially W (**2**), by Brownrigg Moss, to reach the saddle at the head of Far Easedale. At this point, turn E to follow the valley path in comparative shelter and, importantly, with the greatest certainty of homing in on Grasmere.

The path leading up Pike of Carrs

Ridge routes

Gibson Knott →2km/1¼ miles ↓120m/395ft ↑30m/100ft ⏱30min
The path takes off E, traversing eroded peat, before dipping more steeply off Pike of Carrs to a cairn in the depression. The ridge is sufficiently drawn in to give excellent views, although the path's southern bias tends to make

Wild and wonderful – Far Easedale

Easedale the focus of attention. Passing a rock chair to the left, the ridge engages in several switchbacks before it reaches the summit.

Sergeant Man →*3.2km/2 miles* ↓*15m/50ft* ↑*210m/690ft* ⏱*1hr 10min*
En route W, to the saddle between desolate Wythburn Dale and the deeply entrenched Far Easedale, the popular path negotiates some damp ground. The ridge path ignores both valleys, marching due south largely in the company of what remains of the metal estate-boundary stakes, leading via several pleasing pools over Codale Head, and rounding a marsh to climb the obvious, and certainly distinctive, summit knoll.

Steel Fell →*2.4km/1½ miles* ↓*70m/230ft* ↑*90m/295ft* ⏱*1hr*
Leave the summit heading N, and the route soon gets decidedly marshy, especially along the old fence-line. The popular path keeps well to the right, and in so doing enjoys the view into Greenburn Dale down to right. Curving NE, the less well-trod path, near the fence, merges from the left. Saunter on the south side of the two large, oddly nameless tarns. Now going E, follow a fence ascending from the left to the acute corner by the summit cairn.

4 COLD PIKE 701M/2300FT

Climb it from	Wrynose Pass **22** or Wrynose Bottom **23**
Character	Rocky top handily reached from Wrynose Pass
Fell-friendly route	1
Summit grid ref	NY 262 036
Link it with	Crinkle Crags or Pike o'Blisco

Crinkle Crags has two projecting southern ridges, each ending in a flourish at outpost tops. Cold Pike is the more distinct eastern arm, an affiliated rebel crinkle. Across its northern flanks runs the ever-popular path from Wrynose Pass to Crinkle Crags via Red Tarn, yet the fell deserves not to be cold-shouldered.

It makes a delightful quickly-won objective from the top of the pass and its triple-piked summit is especially fun to explore, a place where ideas for easy scrambles seem to proliferate. As a viewpoint, too, its merits are manifest. The Langdale Pikes, Pike o'Blisco and the Coniston group all hold the summiteer's attention.

Three short routes lead up from Wrynose Pass.

↑ *Cold Pike from above Red Tarn*

Ascent from Wrynose Pass 22

Two routes lead up from the top of the pass, Route 1 a little more challenging than the straightforward Route 2.

Via south ridge →2km/1¼ miles ↑310m/1020ft ⏲1hr 20min

1 From the high point of the pass at the Three Shire Stone a well-worn path strikes north. Watch for a cairn indicating a half-left fork. Follow this lesser path. Fording gills and rising onto the easy slopes of a moraine rigg, the path angles up to the prominent skyline knott due west. Pass a banded outcrop with a large cairn to reach a tarn. Keep left of the first two outcrops to reach the summit.

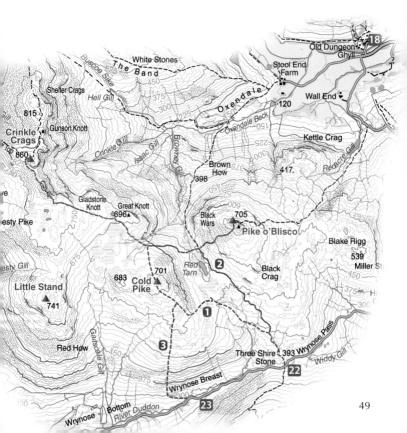

Via Red Tarn → *2.7km/1¾ miles* ↑*310m/1020ft* ⏲*1hr 40min*

2 A simpler route, with obvious paths all the way, keeps to the main path, passing **Red Tarn** on its way to the staggered path junction below Pike o'Blisco. Turn left (west) and cross an exposed patch of red soil (iron oxide). The path rises, giving a fine view down the Browney Gill valley towards the Langdale Pikes. Immediately prior to the first ford, as the path eases onto the moorland plateau, bear up left. A path soon materialises aiming direct for the summit.

Ascent from Wrynose Bottom 23

Via Wrynose Breast → *2km/1¼ miles* ↑*410m/1345ft* ⏲*1hr 20min*

An excellent, if steep, unorthodox ascent

3 A footpath sign points up from a little east of the parking area. Across the ford is a stile in a brief fenced section of an otherwise largely walled enclosure beside the river. Cross this and then follow along the wall west under the slope of the fell. Attention is immediately drawn to a large dark square boulder with a bield wall. Angle up the apron of grass close by. The open gully of the gill harbours delicate flora to intrigue the botanist and, being well endowed with grass, is never a problem in ascent. At the top note the small outcrop to the left where a 3m totem block stands perilously as a pinnacle, waiting for the next shove of ice to render it history. The ground eases and three damp shelves are crossed on the more sedate, pathless trek up the slope to a tarn. Join Route **1** at the tarn.

50

Red Tarn looking to Swirl How and Great Carrs

The summit

The highest ground is without question the fell's finest moment. There are three pronounced rocky rises. Most visitors side-step the southern top and work through to the summit proper. Two cairns rest on opposing outcrops, the northern pile being the true summit, a splendid spot.

Safe descents

With crags immediately east, the sensible choice in mist is NNW (**2**). Meet up with the path from Crinkle Crags, go right, down to the cross-path saddle, then either left for Great Langdale, or right for the road at the top of the Wrynose Pass.

Ridge routes

Crinkle Crags →*2km/1¼ miles* ↓*90m/295ft* ↑*230m/755ft* ⏱*1hr 15min*
Descend NW from the summit to join the path emanating from Red Tarn. Encountering the popular trail go left. For all the restoration work there is still much loose gravel. This path leads over the first crinkle to a wide gap from

where the 'Bad Step' is faced up the rising gully. This obstacle can be avoided by turning left, climbing a loose gravelly path onto Long Top, the summit of Crinkle Crags.

Pike o'Blisco →*2km/1¼ miles* ↓*200m/655ft* ↑*200m/655ft* ⏲*1hr 10min*
Descend NW to join the popular trail. Go right, fording a gill in the saddle and then continue E on a well-marked path which eventually curves N to the summit.

The Langdale Pikes from above Browney Gill

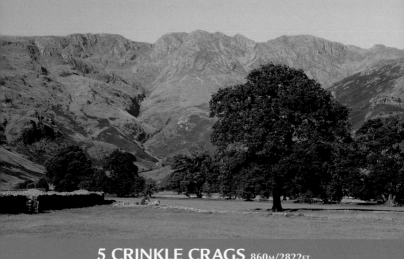

5 CRINKLE CRAGS 860M/2822FT

Climb it from	Old Dungeon Ghyll **18**, Wrynose Pass **22**, Cockley Beck Bridge **24** or Brotherilkeld **25**
Character	Magical sequence of craggy crests, enthralling in sunshine but confusing in mist
Fell-friendly route	2 or 5
Summit grid ref	NY 249 049
Link it with	Bowfell, Little Stand or Cold Pike
Part of	The Great Langdale Round

Seen from the southwest, it is easy to understand why Crinkle Crags is sometimes referred to as Long Top. But viewed from the east, particularly from Pike o'Blisco, you are left in no doubt as to where the popular name derived. Clearly this hunched-up, huddled skyline mass of craggy ground belongs for most in Great Langdale.

The popular circuit heads up the Band from the Old Dungeon Ghyll, trending south from the Three Tarns col. Walkers should be warned. The Bad Step encountered on the southern descent from the main crinkle is more awkward than your average rock problem from this side. It would be better for the novice to embark anti-clockwise, tracking up Oxendale and above Browney Beck to

↑ Crinkle Crags from Wall End   53

meet it from below, where a sane decision can be made whether to take it on, or follow the left-hand variation instead.

But there are so many other ways to climb the crinkles, even from Great Langdale (Routes 1–4). The dale approach from Eskdale (Route 8), via Lingcove Beck, enjoys handsome surroundings and offers three lines to the top (9–11) while another popular route (5) rises up from the Three Shire Stone above Little Langdale and two more from the other end of Wrynose (6–7), all worthy of investigation.

Ascent from Old Dungeon Ghyll 18

From the Old Dungeon Ghyll the irregular skyline has obvious appeal, an inviting coconut shy of craggy tops waiting to be knocked off.

Via the Band →*5km/3 miles* ↑*815m/2675ft* ⏱*3hr 40min*
1 The obvious route follows the **Stool End Farm** road. Pass through the busy farmyard via a gate and take the clear branch right onto the foot of the ridge.

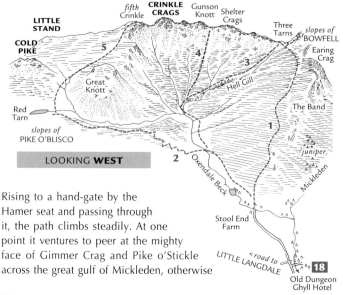

LITTLE STAND

COLD PIKE

fifth Crinkle

CRINKLE CRAGS

Gunson Knott

Shelter Crags

Three Tarns

slopes of BOWFELL

Earing Crag

Great Knott

Hell Gill

5

4

3

The Band

Red Tarn

slopes of PIKE O'BLISCO

1

Juniper

LOOKING WEST

2

Oxendale Beck

Mickleden

Stool End Farm

LITTLE LANGDALE

<road to

18

Old Dungeon Ghyll Hotel

Rising to a hand-gate by the Hamer seat and passing through it, the path climbs steadily. At one point it ventures to peer at the mighty face of Gimmer Crag and Pike o'Stickle across the great gulf of Mickleden, otherwise

Kettle Crag and the elegant peak of Pike o'Blisco rising above Oxendale hold sway during the climb. Thankfully the path has been consolidated to provide firm footing where previously there was a loose unsightly trail. As the path avoids the actual crest, some walkers may be tempted to wander onto the higher ground above **Earing Crag**. The main path roughens underfoot as it reaches up to the **Three Tarns** hause. Don't waste too much time searching for a trio of tarns: there are seldom more than two. Although as you turn south a delightful pool can be found to the left, over peaty ground, jammed tightly in a rock crevice. The path avoids the first minor cairned knott as it mounts **Shelter Crags**. There are several paths, but no one true way. Higher up a reedy pool is passed en route to the gap below **Gunson Knott**, the goal of the direct ascent from Oxendale. Attention is focused on the sequence of little knotts, all of which demand topping, until, at a final gap, **Long Top** hoves into view, with a small ox-bow pool below.

Via Browney Gill →*5km/3 miles* ↑*780m/2560ft* ⏱*3hr 20min*
2 From **Stool End Farm** follow the track into **Oxendale**. Proceed via a gate and sheepfold passage and cross the footbridge. A well-pitched path climbs half-right up the northern slopes of **Pike o'Blisco** onto a rigg above **Browney Gill**. This path continues to the depression where paths meet, short of **Red Tarn**. Here turn west, ford the gill and cross a patch of iron oxide-rich soil

The Bad Step and the easy left-hand side-step onto Long Top

(once used for sheep marking). The way wends on at an easy gradient on a loose gravelly trail. **Great Knott** is ignored by the path, but walkers should not assume this prominent top is without virtue as a viewpoint. The first crinkle you get to (conventionally referred to as the fifth crinkle, as the rising ridge is described from the north) is gained with much relief – firm ground at last! Cross over into the grassy gap with its view back down Great Cove towards

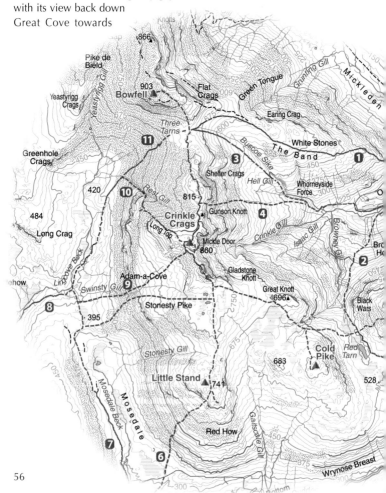

Oxendale. For a sure, unfettered ascent, trend half-left where a simple path mounts onto the western end of **Long Top**. More earnest walkers will see the feature known as the 'Bad Step' as a straightforward scramble but it is not just a matter of putting the right foot first – you need a steady head, too.

Via Hell Gill →*5.5km/3½ miles* ↑*790m/2590ft* ⏱*3hr 40min*

3 The eastern combe attracts more than the occasional walker. Several gills drain into this amphitheatre, but Crinkle Gill is not as appealing as may be thought. Hell Gill is another matter. Follow the path beyond the footbridge, bearing right at the wall-end, and rise onto a contouring path, thus avoiding the awkward path along the edge of the beck. Across the footbridge, the path, with a few pitched sections, rises diagonally. As you approach the handsome mare's tail of **Whorneyside Force**, gingerly cross a landslip to visit the upper fall and pool with its big boulder. Ford the beck at the foot of the **Hell Gill** ravine (strictly no entry!). Mount the left-hand bank where path works have made the path so much sweeter to tread and eradicated a scar too. As the ground eases, look into the ravine and back to Pike o'Blisco: a delightful subject for the camera. The path drifts slightly left of **Buscoe Sike** as it drains into Hell Gill, passing an old fenced area. It only returns to it higher up, as you advance towards **Three Tarns** to join Route **1**.

Direct from Whorneyside Force

→*4.7km/3 miles* ↑*760m/2495ft* ⏱*3hr 25min*

4 From the footbridge below **Whorneyside Force**, wander up the main path only as far as the top of the first paved section to find a bracken-light line up the rigg. Escaping the bracken's clutches altogether, climb the grassy moor with eyes intent on the high gap between the craggy mass of **Gunson Knott** and **Shelter Crags**. Inevitably the ground steepens, but a sure and largely scree-free line can be found. Having tested this route in descent I found walking poles eliminated any need to use my hands. For all the lack of a path the ground is good and firm. Nonetheless, this is not a route to consider in poor conditions.

Ascent from Wrynose Pass 22

A straightforward and rightly popular route

Via Red Tarn →*4.5km/2¾ miles* ↑*505m/1655ft* ⏱*2hr 15min*
5 Walk up northwest from the top of the Wrynose Pass, passing **Red Tarn** on your left before an intersection of paths at a depression. Here, turn west to join Route **2** on the gravelly trail towards **Great Knott**.

Ascent from Cockley Beck Bridge 24 *off map S*

A superb 14km high-level round trip takes in the whole ridge from Little Stand to Esk Pike, returning via Pike de Bield and the south ridge and fording Lingcove Beck below Pianet Knott to enter Mosedale. Route 6 is the straightforward way up; Route 7 the longer, more pathless option.

Via Little Stand →*4km/2½ miles* ↑*690m/2265ft* ⏱*3hr 20min*
6 Ford **Mosedale Beck** just west of Cockley Beck Bridge to a gate/stile (foot-

path sign). After 50m angle quarter-left across damp ground to find a track rising up the bracken bank to the left of another gill. This is all damp stuff, but it brings you to a wall gap and, a little beyond, a stile in the wire fence. Now set a course up the rough slope in the Gaitscale Close enclosure. There is no obvious path up

The Scafells from the ridge

among the boulders, though as you emerge onto the upper pasture shelf as if by magic a path materialises, drawing you up to the apparent saddle between prominent skyline outcrops. Gaining the ridge path, an initial right turn reveals the view from the ridge-end, while the summit cairn lies up to the left, off the more tangible path. The summit of **Little Stand** gives a hint of the attractions of the crinkles, although the intermediate ridge is quite tame. Bear left towards the first crinkle following Route **2** to your destination.

Via Mosedale →4.6km/2¾ miles ↑665m/2180ft ⏱3hr 45min

7 A damp bridleway leads off from the bottom of the Hardknott Pass road threading through **Mosedale** via the dale head moraine rigg, to reach **Swinsty Gill**, **Lingcove Beck** and the path coming from Eskdale. The bridleway splits just short of the intervening rigg-top. Take the right-hand (less travelled) branch. About half a kilometre further on, as it bends to the right, peel off right at the head of Mosedale. Follow this up the steep grassy fellside, passing the outcrops of **Stonesty Pike** on the north side to gain the ridge, latterly skirting a cluster of pools. Turn left (north) with Route **6** to reach the crinkles.

Ascent from Brotherilkeld 25 *off map SW*

The longest approach (8) begins from the foot of Hardknott Pass in Eskdale and leads to three options for gaining the Crinkle Crags ridge: one (pathless) from the west (9), one from the northwest (10) and one from the north (11).

Via Stonesty Pike →*7.2km/4½ miles* ↑*920m/3020ft* ⏱*4hr*
8 Follow the farm track to Brotherilkeld and the subsequent waymarked path, initially tight by the **Esk**. Leaving the shelter of trees traverse enclosures, via gates, onto a regular path where the dale hems in approaching **Lingcove Bridge**. The path to follow keeps up right, just before the sheepfold just before the elegant footbridge. Clamber up on the stony path above the delightful **Lingcove Beck** gorge. Enter the open, wilder aspect of Ling Cove.

9 As **Lingcove Beck** bends north, **Swinsty Gill** enters from the right. This

Crinkle Crags from Pike o'Blisco

may be followed, without a path, keeping up to the right and not within its ravine. The mid-section is suitable for competent scramblers only, as anyone who chances to descend close to the beck will discover: that there is a path at all on the mid-rigg is the result of descending walkers' partial descents and expedient retreats! Turn left at the top with Route **6**.

Via Lingcove Beck →*7.2km/4½ miles* ↑*930m/3050ft* ⏱*4hr 15min*
10 Follow the path beside **Lingcove Beck** further on, heading northeast, slipping over Churn How to reach the stony delta of **Rest Gill**. Strong walkers might like to gain **Long Top** from this point. To do so, don't ford the gill but keep up on the right slope. The steep ground is unrelenting but presents no difficulty in fair weather. Angle up under the outcrops above the ravine. As these abate, go right over boulders below a crag with, for the first time, faint evidence of a path. Cross over the knott to find a clear path in the grass coming in left from the gill and traverse a few boulders

to join the worn path coming up from the gully in **Adam-a-Cove**. Now scramble in relatively easy steps up the broken western bluff-end of Long Top, the path never in doubt.

11 For an easy life, having forded **Rest Gill**, keep with the old path which continues to **Three Tarns** and follow Route **1** south.

The summit

For all its girth, Crinkle Crags is known and adored for its fascinating north to south ridge. One conclusive top after another, each having attracted cairn-builders, each a fine excuse to pause and contemplate the next stage in the exciting crescendo. However, there is no doubting the actual summit. The characteristic Long Top runs east to west, with the principal cairn elevated towards the eastern end. Rock and rough ground is everywhere. The view does justice to the setting – looking east down Crinkle Gill to Oxendale, west to the Scafells or, most handsome, Bowfell due north. This is God's own country… be it revelation or just plain elation, you'll know the feeling!

Safe descents

Tiered cliffs fall to the east of the summit and a mass of steep ground falls south. Elsewhere the ground is simply rough. Two points are of real concern. The Bad Step (see above) is not a route to recommend in poor conditions. Secondly, do not follow the line of cairns chasing off the western bluff-end of Long Top, apparently bound for the Lingcove Beck valley. Clear as they are, this is not a safe line of descent. In fair or foul weather the safe ways are only to be found by sticking to the ridge proper, N to Three Tarns (**1**), turning right for Great Langdale, or south, following the prominent path (**2**) down towards Red Tarn, there choosing between left for Oxendale and the Old Dungeon Ghyll (**2**) or right to Wrynose Pass (**5**), the quickest way to find tarmac.

Ridge routes

Bowfell →2.2km/1½ miles ↓140m/460ft ↑195m/640ft ⏱1hr 15min
The delightful vagaries of the ridge ensure a thoroughly engrossing time N, en route to the Three Tarns hause. A worn trail mounts to the easier ground above Flat Crags and beyond to the summit pyramid.

Little Stand →2km/1¼ miles ↓140m/460ft ↑20m/65ft ⊕25min
Either via the Bad Step, immediately down to the left (with care) or the evasive route, off the top starting W of the summit cairn, traverse the fifth crinkle, break right from the popular path and head due S, with some intervening broken ground on the ridge.

Cold Pike →2km/1¼ miles ↓230m/755ft ↑90m/295ft ⊕40min
From the fifth crinkle follow the popular path SE until, upon fording a gill at the edge of the moor, you can branch up right to the prominent top.

Crinkle Crags summit cairn

6 ESK PIKE 885M/2904FT

Climb it from	Brotherilkeld **25**, Seathwaite **1**, Stonethwaite **2** or Old Dungeon Ghyll **18**
Character	Rocky summit best explored via its south ridge or from adjacent saddles off the Esk Hause bridle-path
Fell-friendly route	1
Summit grid ref	NY 237 075
Link it with	Allen Crags, Bowfell or Great End

Esk Pike is a deceptively extensive fell. Unlike the northern slopes, nipped off neatly beneath Tongue Head, the southern ridge reaches right down to Lingcove Bridge and is quite the meat and matter of good fellwalking. A staggered sequence of rocky headlands draws up to the summit from the Esk, the path largely threading between them on grass as far as Yeastyrigg Crags.

Flanked by two notable high passes, Ore Gap and Esk Hause, Esk Pike is often ignored on ascent and dismissed on descent leaving its special summit for the smarter fellwanderers. With several excellent vantage points and perched between giants of the Lakeland watershed, it is well worth the detour for views over Langstrath, Eskdale and across to the Langdale Pikes.

↑ *Esk Pike from the path to Ore Gap coming off Bowfell*   63

There are four long and lovely routes in from Eskdale (1–4), two good days out from Borrowdale (5–6) and the classic ascent from Mickleden and Great Langdale (7).

Ascent from Brotherilkeld 25 *off map S*

A walk of longing in every respect. Just to set foot on the south ridge requires a 3km march to Lingcove Bridge, followed by a 5km climb. The summit takes an eternity to arrive, but few fellwalking aficionados will begrudge the effort for total immersion in this scenery. But for occasional aircraft overhead you can forget the trappings of modern life entirely.

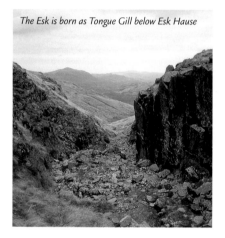

The Esk is born as Tongue Gill below Esk Hause

Via the south ridge →*8.5km/5¼ miles* ↑*800m/2625ft* ⏱*4hr 40min*

1 Follow the farm road to **Brotherilkeld** from the old red telephone box. A permissive path, neatly avoiding the farmyard, wanders tight by the beautifully embowered river. Notice several exposed tree roots indicating how, on occasion, the **River Esk** runs wild. From a hand-gate, the route traverses pasture on an open track, via gates, to enter the more confined section of the valley. Crags loom and

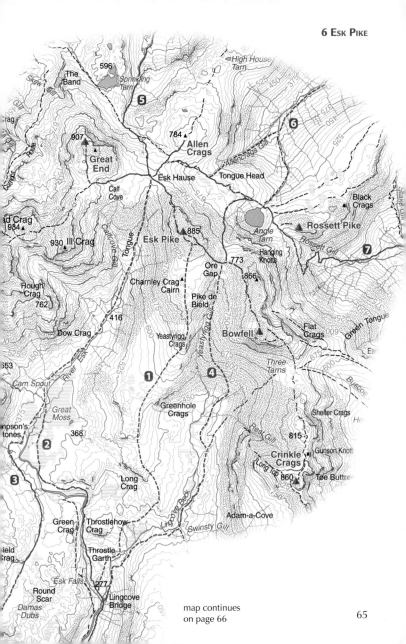

High House Tarn

Skew Gill

596

The Band

Sprinkling Tarn

5

6

907 ▲
Great End

784 ▲
Allen Crags

Esk Hause

Tongue Head

Allencrags Gill

Calf Cove

Calfcove Gill

Black Crags

d Crag
984 ▲

930 ▲ Ill Crag

Tongue

Esk Pike

885 ▲

Angle Tarn

▲ Rossett Pike

Rossett Gill

7

Ore Gap

773

Hanging Knotts

Charnley Crag Cairn

866

Rough Crag
762

Pike de Bield

Flat Crags

Dow Crag

416

Yeastyrigg Crags

Bowfell ▲

Green Tongue

River Esk

653

Cam Spout

Yeastyrigg Gill

1

4

Three Tarns

Ear

Buscoe

Great Moss

368

Greenhole Crags

Shelter Crags

He

mpson's
tones

2

815

Crinkle Crags

Gunson Knott

3

Long Crag

860 ▲

Toe Buttress

Lingcove Beck

Adam-a-Cove

Green Crag

Throstlehow Crag

Swinsty Gill

ield
rag:

Throstle Garth

Round Scar

Esk Falls

277

Damas Dubs

Lingcove Bridge

map continues
on page 66

65

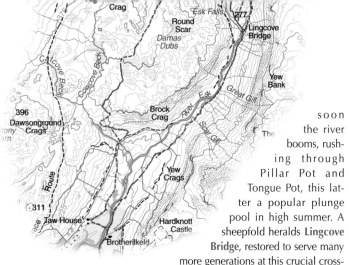

soon the river booms, rushing through Pillar Pot and Tongue Pot, this latter a popular plunge pool in high summer. A sheepfold heralds **Lingcove Bridge**, restored to serve many more generations at this crucial crossing. Upstream, Lingcove Beck fights through a series of narrow, stepped rocky channels, finishing at a delightful fall in view from the bridge. Follow the main path leading northwest from the bridge, then take the right-hand fork nearing the brow, a tangible path weaving through the bracken above the lower outcrop of **Throstle Garth**. The path comes close to **Lingcove Beck**. Watch for the smart diversion half-left, onto the fell, rising over the grassy rigg to pass through the low, broken wall that once defined Throstle Garth. The ridge path is no wider than a sheep path, so a keen eye is needed to keep it underfoot. Follow the rising grassy ridge over the shoulder between **Long Crag** and Pianet Knott, slanting ever upward above **Greenhole** and **Yeastyrigg Crags**. Outcrops make it difficult to keep a consistent path. Clambering onto the higher ridge, divert left to the prominent cairn on the neat peak of **Pike de Bield**. The endeavour now eases. Another larger cairn is found above **Charnley Crag** before you reach the spine of the fell and bear up left to the summit.

Via Great Moss or Cowcove →9km/5½ miles ↑790m/2590ft ⏲5hr

There are two dale routes to consider. Choose Route 2 if the river is down and Route 3 in wetter conditions.

2 The more appealing approach follows Route **1** as far as **Lingcove Bridge** and then continues on with the **River Esk**, on the popular path for Cam Spout.

Ford the river at **Great Moss** and walk upstream on the west bank. Mount the rigg to thread the ravine of **Tongue Gill** to **Esk Hause**. The ravine section half-way up may be awash, requiring evasive action up to the left. Turn sharp right at the hause to climb the northwest ridge to the summit.

3 If the river seems high use the Cowcove zig-zag route. Follow the farm road to **Brotherilkeld** from the red telephone kiosk, guided left of Brotherilkeld

ESK PIKE

Esk Hause

Ore Gap

slopes of GREAT END

Pike de Bield

slopes of BOWFELL

Yeastyrigg Crags

slopes of SCAFELL PIKE

High Gait Crags

1

Green Hole

4

Cam Spout

slopes of CRINKLE CRAGS

slopes of SCAFELL

Great Moss

2

Lingcove Beck

River Esk

Throstlehow

slopes of SLIGHT SIDE

Esk Falls

Damas Dubs

Lingcove Bridge

Heron Crag

3

Brock Crag

Cowcove zig-zags

slopes of HARD KNOTT

Taw House

farm-track

Brotherilkeld

Hardknott Pass >

26

River Esk

25

<BOOT

Whahouse Bridge

LOOKING **NORTHEAST**

farmyard to a hand-gate, and, a matter of a few metres on, go left, crossing the wooden footbridge spanning the wonderfully tree-shaded **River Esk**. Traverse the pasture, with a wall on your right, to a ladder-stile entering the farmyard at **Taw House**. Leave the farmyard by the gate at its northern end and follow the lane to a gate, thereafter on an open track, via two gateways, to a gate/ladder-stile at a sheepfold. A clear track continues to Scale Bridge, crossing the cascades of Scale Gill. The footpath is signed further along the track, but an intermediary path takes a cavalier direct diagonal line up to the **Cowcove zig-zags** from the bridge. The footpath track follows the west side of the valley. Watch for the acute turn left up through the bracken – the path is clear enough. Higher, the zig-zags afford a view into the **Cowcove Beck** ravine before entering the first of two marshy hollows. Keep to the dry western edge, crossing a plank over **Damas Dubs**, the natural drainage for the two hollows to reach the sheepfold complex beneath Cam Crag. Skirt the marsh below **Cam Spout**, **Dow Crag** and Little Narrowcove in order to reach the foot of **Tongue Gill** and join Route **2**.

Via Ore Gap →9km/5½ miles ↑790m/2590ft ⏱5hr

A fine route diverging from the Esk to follow Lingcove Beck up to Ore Gap.

4 Take Route **1** to reach **Lingcove Bridge** and then carry on to the right of **Lingcove Beck**. Rough at first, a narrow path 'comes round the mountain' to enter the combe over the saddle from Mosedale and soon arrives beneath

Adam-a-Cove. Divert from the well-marked path bound for **Three Tarns**. As it shapes to cross Churn How, contour into the bowl of Ling Cove directly beneath **Bowfell**. Some of the ling (heather) persists, notable in the Lingcove gorge, forming frilly edges beyond the reach of nibbling Herdwicks.

Cross-wall below Esk Hause

The path avoids the lower section of **Yeastyrigg Gill**, which is far too stony. It ascends the rigg on the midriff of Bowfell then, curving left over the brow, keeps above a prominent erratic boulder, in the end coming close to the gill by stony hops to reach **Ore Gap**. Turn left (NW) to walk up to the summit.

Ascent from Seathwaite 1 *off map N* or Stonethwaite 2 *off map NE*

Few walkers set sail from Borrowdale with Esk Pike a prime objective but it is no less a course to set for that.

Via Seathwaite and Ruddy Gill →5.2km/3¼ miles ↑780m/2560ft ⏱4hr 25min

5 The more direct route begins from Seathwaite. Follow the tread of a million soles to Stockley Bridge and then turn south climbing via **Grains and Ruddy Gills** to join the path rising from Sty Head. When that path forks, bear right to reach **Esk Hause**, with the northwest ridge path onto Esk Pike beckoning.

Via Langstrath and Ore Gap →8.2km/5 miles ↑790m/2590ft ⏱4hr 50min

A great excuse to explore Langstrath to its ultimate extent.

6 From Stonethwaite, keep to the west-side path in Langstrath to the Tray Dub footbridge, cross the footbridge at the foot of Stake Beck and follow **Langstrath Beck**, with the high fellsides progressively hemming in the path. Ford Angletarn Gill – easier said than done when it's in spate. The subsequent fellside, running up the headstream of **Allencrags Gill**, is rough, with just the hint of a path on the steep ground rising to **Tongue Head**. The popular path joined, with some relief, go right, to the cross-wall wind shelter. Slant up leftward to **Esk Hause** and onto the northwest ridge to the summit.

Ascent from Old Dungeon Ghyll **18** *off map E*

A clear and classic approach

Via Rossett Gill →*6km/3¾ miles* ↑*785m/2575ft* ⏱*3hr 30min*
7 From the Old Dungeon Ghyll, the regular path climbs out of Mickleden via **Rossett Gill**, on a solidly pitched, double zig-zag trail bringing most walkers to **Angle Tarn** with Bowfell or Scafell Pike their principal objectives. Continue past the tarn to the saddle south of **Allen Crags**. Turn southwest by the cross-wall shelter to rise to **Esk Hause** and step up the inviting northwest ridge to the Pike on the well-marked rocky path.

The summit

The south top is fundamentally rock, the north top a looser affiliation, surmounted by a more compact cairn. The eye-catching pale rock, which from a distance has the appearance of chalk but is in fact a flaky glaze, is most prevalent on the south side. The central situation on the

The summit

main ridge, encircling the great wilderness of upper Eskdale and high above upper Langstrath, lends the summit special qualities as a viewpoint. There are several subsidiary vantages either side of the summit worth finding. Descend north a matter of 150m. If you peer down a gully into upper Langstrath you can see Glaramara. While on the other side of the summit find the bird's-eye

Angle Tarn from below Ore Gap

view down the same scarp to admire Angle Tarn backed by Rossett Pike and the Langdale Pikes. Pike de Bield at the top of the south ridge is the better stance for upper Eskdale.

Safe descents

The best objective is Ore Gap. Follow the ridge path SE from the summit (**4**). At the Ore Gap depression turn left, N, down a rough but plain path. Join the path from Esk Hause (**7**) winding on down to the outflow of Angle Tarn. Ford the gill and continue SE bound for Rossett Gill, with its pitched zig-zags, and Mickleden, for the shelter of Great Langdale. If you are intent on return-ing to Borrowdale, NNW from the summit, the ridge path (**2**) descends to Esk Hause, a notoriously confusing place in mist. From here continue down in the same sense to take the path heading NNE down Ruddy Gill (**5**). (If, instead, you reach the cross-wall shelter, a key landmark, take a new bearing NW to follow another path back to the same junction at the head of Ruddy Gill.)

Ridge routes

Allen Crags →1.6km/1 mile ↓170m/560ft ↑70m/230ft ⏱25min
To embark upon the Glaramara ridge, descend the NW ridge to Esk Hause and slant right, passing down by the cross-wall to the saddle. Continue on the stony trail, easily climbing NE to the summit.

Bowfell →1.6km/1 mile ↓100m/330ft ↑120m/395ft ⏱35min
Descend the SE ridge to Ore Gap. Continue on an oft stony trail which mounts steadily S, only really getting onto the ridge proper at the brink of the scree gully between Bowfell Buttress and Cambridge Crag. The final rocky crest of the fell ensues. Step up SE, veering off the line of the diagonal shelf path. This is a proper fell-top with plenty of stony seats for that all-important breather.

Great End →2km/1¼ miles ↓125m/410ft ↑160m/525ft ⏱45min
Descend the NW ridge to Esk Hause. A string of cairns guides to the all-too-apparent path across the broad depression into Calf Cove. The excessively boulder-ridden E slope of Great End should be given short shrift. Slant up left beyond the bield wall with the popular path to Scafell Pike. Take a right-hand turn due N. Where the stony ground eases follow the gently rising broad ridge to the summit, almost devoid of rough ground.

Esk Pike from Great End

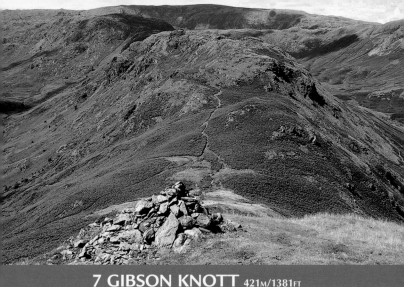

7 GIBSON KNOTT 421M/1381FT

Climb it from	Mill Bridge 5 or Grasmere 6–9
Character	Middle summit along the fascinating Helm Crag ridge between Far Easedale and Greenburn Dale
Fell-friendly route	3
Summit grid ref	NY 317 100
Link it with	Calf Crag or Helm Crag
Part of	The Greenburn Horseshoe

Fells come in many guises. Some are solitary summits while others, like Gibson Knott, are characterful components of a greater whole. The greater whole in question here is the triple-topped ridge dividing Far Easedale from Greenburn Dale. Iconic Helm Crag sits to its southeast and lonely Calf Crag to the northwest. The southern slopes are rough and uninviting, with Horn Crag, the one major feature, tucked under the summit. The still-steep northern slopes are, thankfully, accessible.

As a ridge walk the three tops make up an undulating roller-coaster ride that should put a smile on any fellwalker's face – and the usual array of excellent views rewards anyone who stops to appreciate them.

↑ *Gibson Knott from Helm Crag*

There is but one line of approach from Far Easedale venturing to the Bracken Hause saddle below Helm Crag (Route 4). From Greenburn Dale, to the north, there are three comfortable lines (1–3).

Ascent from Mill Bridge 5

Two less-travelled trails start in peaceful Greenburn Dale.

Via Bracken Hause →*2km/1¼ miles* ↑*335m/1100ft* ⏱*1hr 50min*
1 Follow the minor road down over the **River Rothay**, bearing right by Ghyll Foot to reach the drive access to Helmside. Ascend the metalled lane, via its cattle grids, to the gate beyond Turn Howe. Go forward along the level track passing through a gate, with **Green Burn Beck** close down to the left. Bear left to cross the wooden footbridge above the first waterfall. The path climbs the pasture to cross the lane via facing hand-gates, then climbs directly up the short turf slope to Bracken Hause, the saddle depression below Helm Crag. Turn right. To begin with, the path runs along the far (southern) flank of the ridge, with a bird's-eye view over Stythwaite Steps into Far Easedale, before pitching back up onto the knobbly crest. Watch for the summit cairn, as the path turns a 'blind eye' at the critical moment.

Via Greenburn Dale →*3.2km/2 miles* ↑*350m/1150ft* ⏱*2hr 25min*
2 Pass the bridge where Route **1**branches left on your left to keep to the track via a second gate and short lane, and pass above a more impressive waterfall, made all the more picturesque by the larch spinney and attendant ice-smoothed outcrop. The adjacent wall is lost, and the track becomes a little less certain until, breaking through the moraine, it encounters the large,

The summit looking to Steel Fell and Helvellyn

shallow basin of Greenburn Bottom. High to the right Blakerigg Crag presides over a lovely wild scene, the hollow once filled by a tarn. Comparable shallow pools adorn the flat ridge that forms the northwestern headwall to this truncated dale. The path veers left to cross the stepping-stones. Turn left a matter of 30m downstream before bearing right to mount the obvious rounded grassy rigg, without a hint of a path. Climb, avoiding the skyline crags to your left, and join the ridge path at a marshy depression. Go left to reach the top after a tilted slab.

3 Alternatively, from the stepping-stones on Route **2**, bear right on a pleasing green way by an unusual triangular sheepfold built against three large boulders. The casual stroll is interrupted at a very modest six-stone cairn, and from here the path heads uphill. Only after stepping over a marshy patch does the ascent ease onto a weaving trail that rises to the twin-dip saddle on the ridge. Ahead, across Far Easedale, Deer Bield Crag is the striking cliff feature on the shadowy northern flank of Tarn Crag and up to the right, the false summit of Pike of Carrs leads the eye westward up the ridge towards Calf Crag. Guided by the left-hand of two

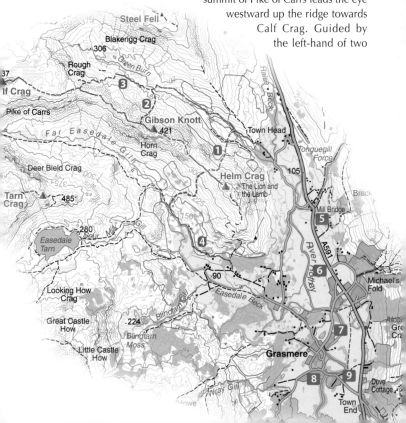

Blakerigg Crag from Greenburn Bottom

cairns, head east along the ridge. After some 100m spot an alcove 'throne' built into a ruckle of rocks to the left of the path. The ridge is entertainingly rocky, though there is one peaty interlude you cannot avoid. As the path

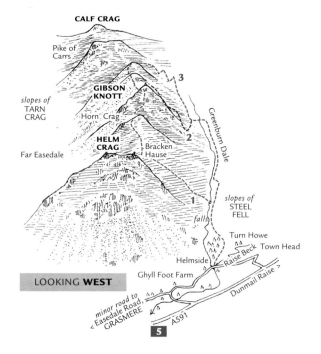

LOOKING WEST

5

comes above a small crag watch for the summit cairn close on the left. It is easy to miss when attention is fixed on maintaining a steady step!

Ascent from Grasmere 6–9

Straightforward but steep this route starts from the centre of the village

Via Bracken Hause →3.5km/2¼ miles ↑340m/1115ft ⏱2hr

4 Follow either Easedale Road or the adjacent fenced path beside the hay meadow to cross Goody Bridge. Now enter Easedale. Beyond Oak Lodge the road leads via a gate through the midst of a meadow, and becomes confined once more at Little Parrock. Facing the lane approach to Brimmer Head Farm keep right, signposted 'Far Easedale & Helm Crag'. A cobbled path rises, by a large dilapidated house, to a metal gate.

From the metal gate go left with the bridle-path, again initially flanked by woodland. The rough, tracked lane passes a vernacular barn to come alongside **Far Easedale Gill**. As the right-hand wall bears up to the right, follow suit. There is little early evidence of a path, but one does materialise, winding up onto a knoll to mount the steep bracken slope. Pass a lone thorn at a spring to reach the saddle of Bracken Hause. Turn left with Route **1** to follow the ridge to the summit.

The summit

There are several contending knobby knolls at the top but only one summit cairn. The view is everything, especially over the wild bowl of Far Easedale. However, there is much else to enjoy. Helm Crag seems lowly backed by the might of the Helvellyn range. To the north rises the craggy face of Steel Fell and southwards the Coniston Fells lie beyond Blea Rigg. But it is to the rocky bulk of Codale Head that most attention will be given, with Harrison Stickle and Pavey Ark making guest appearances.

Safe descents

Hold to the popular ridge path. If the need to leave the ridge is urgent then Bracken Hause (E) provides steep but sure lines to the foot of either Greenburn Dale for Town Head (**1**, north) or Far Easedale for Grasmere (**4**, south). There are two further reliable ways into Greenburn Dale – firstly from the first deep depression west of the summit, a pathless grass line (**2**) down to the stepping-stones, and secondly by the old shepherds' path further west (**3**), immediately before the climb to Pike of Carrs.

Ridge routes

Calf Crag →*2km/1¼ miles* ↓*30m/100ft* ↑*120m/395ft* ⏱*25min*
The ridge path NW is clear cut, only becoming taxing with the climb to Pike of Carrs, and from then swathes of eroded peat lead to the summit outcrop. The views en route, particularly to Deer Bield Crag, are excellent.

Helm Crag →*1.6km/1 mile* ↓*90m/295ft* ↑*100m/330ft* ⏱*40min*
The path dips SE from the summit with the main path trending onto the southern flank, while a slightly more taxing path continues along the ridge proper. If this has virtue, then it is as a means of side-stepping the inevitable drudgery

Gibson Knott from Tarn Crag overtopped by Seat Sandal and Fairfield

of engaging with large walking parties. Helm Crag forms such a wonderful culmination to the ridge. The path slips straight across Bracken Hause and climbs directly to the foot of the massive jagged summit outcrop… which only leaves you with the decision whether to climb it or not!

8 GREAT END 907m/2976ft

Climb it from	Seathwaite **1** or Wasdale Head Village Green **28**
Character	A commanding viewpoint, above a forbidding northern rim of crags, the best place to survey upper Borrowdale
Fell-friendly route	2
Summit grid ref	NY 227 084
Link it with	Esk Pike or Scafell Pike
Part of	The Roof of England

Whether viewed from Wasdale Head or Borrowdale, Great End is clearly the abrupt conclusion of the high plateau, linking naturally to the southwest to Broad Crag and Ill Crag. From Sprinkling Tarn, its shadow-darkened north face, etched with gullies and renowned for its winter ice climbs, is seen to perfection.

Worthy objective though it is, for fellwalkers as much as climbers, if you stand at the brink of this sumptuous north-facing cliff to enjoy the uninhibited views you will most likely be alone with your elation. And despite its outward ferocity, there are wonderful ways to discover Great End, up dramatic ravines and over ancient packhorse routes or perhaps following in the footsteps of thirsty travellers heading over from Borrowdale to partake of a pint at the Wasdale Head Inn and stumble back in the dark?

↑ *Great End from Sprinkling Tarn*   79

The fell is often added to expeditions from Great Langdale, conveniently bolted onto the journeys to and from Scafell Pike. The primary lines up to Styhead Pass and Sprinkling Tarn, however, are a gradual out-and-back up Lingmell Beck from Wasdale (6) and the two packhorse routes (1–3) from Borrowdale. There you can choose from three contrasting lines to the summit.

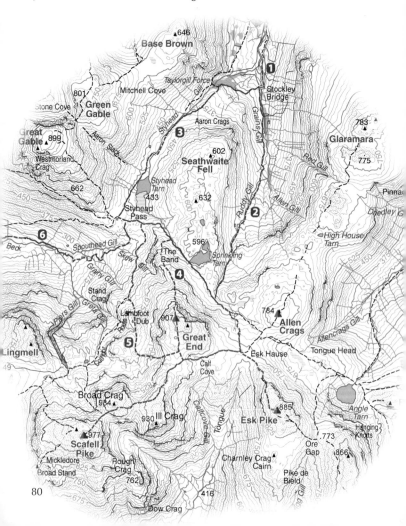

Ascent from Seathwaite 1 *off map N*

The lynch-pin for ascents from Borrowdale is Stockley Bridge.

1 The valley track leads from the farm, via gates, to this elegant single-span packhorse bridge, constructed stoutly on bare rocks, where **Grains Gill** forces through a modest but quite beautiful ravine, especially exciting when the gill is in spate. The gate on the west side is the point where two dale routes divide.

Via Grains Gill →*4.7km/3 miles* ↑*790m/2590ft* ⏲*3hr 45min*

Without question, this route is the easiest route to the top.

2 This path has become the high-road to Esk Hause thanks to intensive pitching works. It crosses a footbridge as **Ruddy Gill** makes its final flight down a

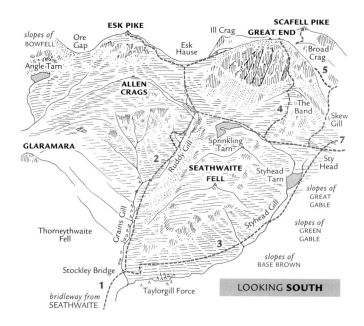

Stockley Bridge

cleft to a secretive fall and a fuming waters-meet with **Allen Gill**, careering on as **Grains Gill**. At the second minor gill crossing you can drift up the rigg half-left onto the prominent shelf. This is the older packhorse route and makes an interesting soft staircase alternative to the hard pitching, If you do, then skirt the marshy ground on the shelf to the west side and link back to the modern trail. The upper section of Ruddy Gill runs through a deep ravine with some trees managing to grow unhindered by the Herdwicks!

Ford the gill to join the path ascending from **Sprinkling Tarn**, taking the right-hand fork to reach **Esk Hause** above the cross-wall shelter. Leading into the shallow combe of **Calf Cove**, a ceaseless flow of walkers ensures a clear path with a superfluity of cairns to boot. As the ground eases above this damp hollow, branch right heading north up the broad semi-pasture ridge to the summit, thereby completely side-stepping the boulder-infested east slope.

Via Styhead Pass →5.5km/3½ miles ↑800m/2625ft ⏱3hr 25min

The setting of this ancient route is a stirring one and the popular rocky path is unmistakable.

3 The path winds up from the gate beyond **Stockley Bridge**, via a rock-step to a gate in the intake wall below Black Waugh, a broad, ice-smoothed grim-looking rock-face. The path continues, gradually easing in gradient though not necessarily in its roughness. Cross a footbridge and walk forward to glance by the western shore of **Styhead Tarn** – a popular high-level camp site. Arrive at the Mountain Rescue stretcher box at **Styhead Pass**, a natural rendezvous point. Go left, setting course for **Esk Hause**. The path, never in doubt, crosses the outflow of **Sprinkling Tarn**. Cross a low saddle to join Route **2** by Ruddy Gill.

Via the Band →5.5km/3½ miles ↑800m/2625ft ⏱3hr 30min

This ridge is nowhere near as intimidating a climb as might be thought at first sight.

4 Leave the route to **Esk Hause**, when you reach outcrops on the slopes of Seathwaite Fell to the left and after a stretch of pitching. Climb to a small col, as a grassy trod winds on up the ridge. The impressive Spouthead scarp close to the right gives magnificent views to **Lingmell**. A shallow gully marks the top of **Skew Gill**, a point of further divide. The direct, mild scramble continues upward with a certain inevitable vagueness. Never fear, there is a simple line which draws up to a gully providing a fine view to Cust's Gully, identified by its huge chockstone. This gully, itself a demanding scramble, is not recommended, so it's best to give it a miss unless you have the necessary climbing skills. Instead tackle the final stretch of bouldery slope to reach the top. Make a point of skirting the cliff edge to see the top of Central and Cust's Gully and the dramatic fell arena below.

Via Lambfoot Dub →4.5km/2¾ miles ↑805m/2640ft ⏱3hr 40min

This route starts with the busy Corridor route but slips away, off-path, to find the tranquil Lambfoot Dub and a quiet western approach to the summit.

Lambfoot Dub

The view from the top of Central Gully

5 Set off from the **Styhead Pass** stretcher box, heading up the Esk Hause path onto the first rise to branch right, to cross the vestige of a short wall, dip and contour to the mouth of the **Skew Gill** ravine. At Skew Gill, frequently a dry jumble of stones, mount the opposing slope and climb on, slipping through a short rock cutting. The pitched staircase is clear ahead. When you spot a round-headed knoll high above, branch off the **Corridor Route**. Clamber up the predominantly grassy slope, slipping behind the knoll to find **Lambfoot Dub**. The pool is surprisingly clear and deep, a lovely spot to rest alone, blissfully gazing across to Great Gable, well above the chattering trekkers on the Corridor. Traverse into the nameless combe behind Round How, joining the headstream of **Greta Gill** which curves up left to its source at the natural weakness in the scarp. This gives steep, but simple, access to the saddle above and thereby the summit up to the left (north).

Ascent from Wasdale Head Village Green 28 *off map* W

Via Styhead Pass → *5km/3 miles* ↑*830m/2725ft* ⏱*3hr30min*

Great End captivates the attention on the walk up Lingmell Beck from Burnthwaite, the high, rugged skyline a tempting call to arms – or to legs!

6 Leave the car park and follow the lane to Burnthwaite. Pass to the left of the farm buildings to a gate. Keep right. The obvious way heads on between varying walls, via a gate, to cross a footbridge spanning Gable Beck. Soon you face a choice of routes to Sty Head, both equally sound. The standard route sticks religiously to the rising path which passes through a hand-gate before reaching scree. The smart route lies up the valley. (Alternatively take the scree on the way up and return along the valley for a little variety.) Either bear off as bracken begins to encroach or wait a further hundred metres to find a clear path slanting down to the hand-gate near the foot of a wall. Keep alongside **Lingmell Beck**, fording the stream just after the confluence with **Piers Gill**. A clear green trail winds up the rigg, then fords a gill to the left. Slant across the next rigg to ford **Spouthead Gill**, then zig-zag up to **Styhead Pass**.

The summit

Two tops of almost identical height vie for pre-eminence. The northwest cairn is further forward and so it better commands the northern prospect, although the Langdale Pikes and Lingmoor Fell are hidden from view from here.

Safe descents

Walk S to the depression, a little over a quarter of a mile distant, to meet up with the path from Scafell Pike. Switch sharp left in the company of this popular trail (**2**) descending Calf Cove to Esk Hause. **Do not** walk south from this point. Find the cross-wall. It is only a short stride NE to Allen Crags hause – the 'false' Esk Hause – from here. Crossing the saddle E–W, a regular path leads to safety: E to **Angle Tarn** and Rossett Gill for Great Langdale and W for **Ruddy Gill** (**2**) and Borrowdale, or further to Styhead Pass for Wasdale Head (**6**).

Ridge routes

Esk Pike →*2km/1¼ miles* ↓*160m/525ft* ↑*125m/410ft* ⏱*30min*
Descend S to the depression, with minimal hindrance from rocks or boulders. Join the path from Scafell Pike switching left, E. Descend Calf Cove following the line of cairns to Esk Hause. Cross straight over, mounting the well-marked path up the NW ridge.

Scafell Pike →*2.5km/1½ miles* ↓*100m/330ft* ↑*185m/605ft* ⏱*40min*

Descend S to the depression to join the path emerging from Calf Cove. Continue SW, soon encountering an awkward and unavoidable section of boulders. The ridge narrows, succeeded by a mild interval of gravelly trail slipping into the dip between Ill Crag and Broad Crag, and then, over the east shoulder of the latter, boulder-hopping resumes with a vengeance! Descend to Broadcrag Col and climb the facing narrow greatly hammered ridge, loose stones in abundance. Eventually matters ease and the walled summit stand hoves into view. The best shelters from the wind are to be found on the east side, over to the left as you reach the plateau.

Looking down on the chockstone in Cust's Gully

9 HARRISON STICKLE 736M/2415FT

Climb it from	Stickle Ghyll **17**
Character	Focal summit at the midst of the Langdale Pikes group
Fell-friendly route	2
Summit grid ref	NY 282 074
Link it with	Loft Crag, Pavey Ark, Pike o'Stickle or Thunacar Knott
Part of	The Langdale Pikes

The Langdale Pikes are up there with Skiddaw and Great Gable as Lakeland icons. If you arrive in Great Langdale by the winding road from Elterwater there is a point where you turn the corner out of Chapel Stile and suddenly comprehend the majesty of the Langdale Pikes. It's an unforgettable moment that any mountain-loving visitor must relish. Harrison Stickle is the focal point, lord and master of this noble group of fells.

The four 'pikes' are Harrison Stickle, Loft Crag, Pike o'Stickle and Pavey Ark, with Thunacar Knott as back-stop. The craggy head of Harrison Stickle throws down steep slopes to Stickle Tarn. Boasting its own extra little peak in Pike How, the mighty southeastern ridge reaches down to the valley between Dungeon and Stickle Ghylls. The invitation is surely irresistible.

↑ *Harrison Stickle and Tarn Crag*   87

Three contrasting routes up from the valley are described here, in descending order of popularity, but the summit is also easily reached from any of the other Pikes.

Ascent from Stickle Ghyll 17

Via Stickle Ghyll →*2.5km/1½ miles* ↑*640m/2100ft* ⏱*2hr*

The ultra-popularity of the Langdale Pikes has ensured a plethora of paths but Routes 1 and 2 make a natural, albeit popular circuit.

1 Go either directly up the bridle-path from the hotel or ascend from Stickle Ghyll car park information shelter. The paths meet up by the fenced gap and follow the paved path beside **Stickle Ghyll**. Cross the footbridge and rise to a

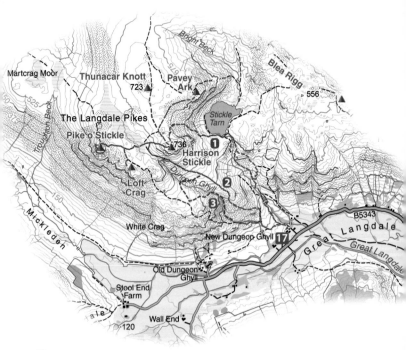

stile. Keep to the right-hand side of the valley, winding through a fenced area intended to shield the slope from erosion.

The path forks, with pitching on both right and left paths. The popular route keeps left above the gill. Higher up, after a rock-step, this path fords the gill and arrives at the dam before **Stickle Tarn**. The right-hand variant path zig-zags as a stone stair to a further fork, where it bears up left and climbs over the shoulder of the intermediate outcrop below **Tarn Crag**, thereby linking with the Stickle Ghyll path and completing the ascent to the tarn.

Ahead is the massive crag of Pavey Ark frowning down on the cool, dark waters of Stickle Tarn, and high to the left rises Harrison Stickle. Go left on the obvious path. Work up the slope to the right of the buttresses. On meeting the contouring path from Pavey Ark, head left, on a choice of two paths, to the very top. The left-hand path is marginally easier.

Via Pike How →*2.5km/1½ miles* ↑*640m/2100ft* ⏱*2hr*

2 The Pike How route leads off left from the fence-gap where the paths from the hotel and the car park meet, rises to a hand-gate and turns right, passing a seat to a stile. Keep the wall on your right, and do not ford **Dungeon Ghyll**. The well-marked path bears left mounting the steep slope in steady stages. Much of it has been re-engineered to cope with the inevitable heavy foot traffic. Many walkers use this as their return leg after the ascent via Stickle Ghyll. Climbing up to the saddle behind **Pike How**, make the move right to stand on top. It is a super viewpoint. (Note: A minor path advances north from Pike How along the rim of the slope on a right-hand curve to reach the Stickle Tarn dam. This path would make an honourable retreat, having ascended Stickle Ghyll only to find the higher fells consumed in cloud.)

The main path proceeds across the open pasture aiming west-northwest for the high shoulder above the deep upper gorge of Dungeon Ghyll. The aggressive slope beneath Harrison Crag affords the path little room, so take your time and watch your footing, as there is loose ground to negotiate. On entering Harrison Combe come to the path junction above the peat-hopping stepping-stones. Either turn sharp right – this route has a rock-step halfway up – or curve round to the right to approach the summit from the northwest without such an obstacle.

Via Dungeon Ghyll →*2.7km/1¾ miles* ↑*640m/2100ft* ⏱*2hr 25min*

Bogbean in Harrison Combe

For those attuned to wild ravines Dungeon Ghyll has an aura that is at the same time forbidding and fabulously attractive. The lower section, shrouded in bracken and trees, is a tight gorge, wherein lurks the actual dungeon. There is no way through.

3 The route branches from Route **2** fording **Dungeon Ghyll** on the re-engineered path on course for **Loft Crag.**

However, at the next easing of the ravine above **Dungeon Force** you can cautiously enter, being careful not to trip on tree roots as you do. Scramble over the mid-gill rocks to follow the right bank up to the first mare's-tail waterfall. Scramble dexterously up the right-hand outcrop. The scenery is superb. Keep to the right bank until forced over to the left side, and climb up through the large boulders to reach the upper fall. Here is a thunderous scene, the water crashing into a pool before finally spilling to the gill floor. The exit is the unlikely looking 'sinister' (left-hand) gully, but a simple, safe scramble leads onto the tame fell pasture. Hold to the trod bearing right

Harrison Stickle from Mill Gill (photo: Peter Savin)

from the popular path to Loft Crag and angle gently down to ford Dungeon Ghyll in this tame intermediary phase. The path quickly joins Route **2**.

The summit

Given good visibility it would be hard not to enjoy a visit to this place. There are cairns on the north and south tops, the former being the actual summit. Rock abounds, with the most threatening on the southern rim, so be wary. Pavey Ark is impressive and its relationship to Stickle Tarn seen here at its best. The blue ribbon of Windermere draws the eye east with the Low Wood Hotel gleaming white on its far shore. It's a wonderful spot from which to witness how the fells rise from the Silurian south and east to a heroic volcanic girdle of high fells crowding above Great Langdale.

Safe descents

Just make sure you leave the summit N – there is nothing but peril to the south. Paths are well enough marked by constant use. The steep, rough descent to Stickle Tarn (**1**) is sheltered from a western breeze. The easier route takes the path trending N, as if to Thunacar Knott, and follows a left-curving line from west to south (black line on map) into Harrison Combe. The narrow trod above the upper gorge of Dungeon Ghyll (**2**) demands care. Beyond, the way is simple, heading southeast to round Pike How to the right.

The airy summit cairn

Ridge routes

Loft Crag →0.4km/¼ mile ↓105m/345ft ↑60m/195ft ⏲20min
Two popular paths lead either W, with a rock-step to carefully negotiate, or N, curving left over easier slopes down to the stepping-stones. Cross the large boulders to help avoid further erosion in the peaty hollow of Harrison Combe. Take the first path left, then angle right on the path mounting the prominent ridge to the cairn.

Pavey Ark →0.8km/½ mile ↓60m/200ft ↑10m/35ft ⏲30min
Either slip down the N path which contours just below the edge over rough ground, or keep to the ridge via the NW path, passing a rock tor before drifting right to join a more definite path. The coarse rocks, obviously abrasive, are a fascinating feature of this locale and may tempt many a photographer to reach for his or her camera, seeking to use the textured rocks as foreground subjects. Cross the wall to reach the cairnless summit.

Pike o'Stickle →*0.8km/½ miles* ↓*105m/345ft* ↑*75m/245ft* ⏱*40min*
Follow the Loft Crag route to the stepping-stones in Harrison Combe, then
continue W on the worn path to the base of the summit stack. It's hands-on-
rock all the way to the top – a compulsive climb to a stunning, scenic station.

Thunacar Knott →*0.8km/½ miles* ↓*60m/195ft* ↑*45m/150ft* ⏱*25min*
Take the NW path, dipping to skirt to the left of the rock tor. Not being on a
main ascent route the path is less than convincing. The first cairn is the summit, and the cairn beyond the pool, elsewhere cited as the summit, is several
feet lower.

Gimmer Crag backed by Harrison Stickle from Great Knott

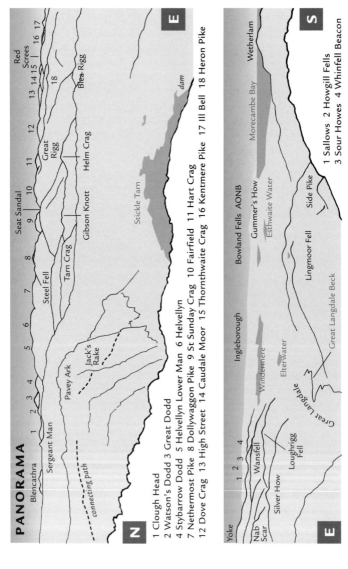

PANORAMA

N

E

1 Clough Head
2 Watson's Dodd 3 Great Dodd
4 Stybarrow Dodd 5 Helvellyn Lower Man 6 Helvellyn
7 Nethermost Pike 8 Dollywaggon Pike 9 St Sunday Crag 10 Fairfield 11 Hart Crag
12 Dove Crag 13 High Street 14 Caudale Moor 15 Thornthwaite Crag 16 Kentmere Pike 17 Ill Bell 18 Heron Pike

S

E

1 Sallows 2 Howgill Fells
3 Sour Howes 4 Whinfell Beacon

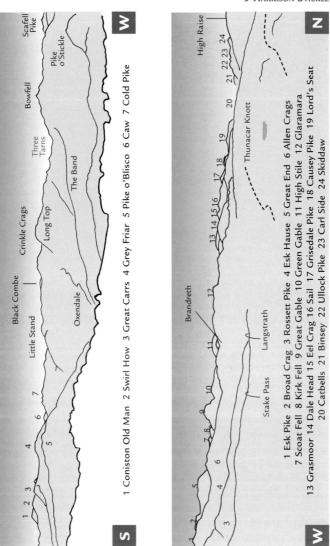

1 Coniston Old Man 2 Swirl How 3 Great Carrs 4 Grey Friar 5 Pike o'Blisco 6 Caw 7 Cold Pike

1 Esk Pike 2 Broad Crag 3 Rossett Pike 4 Esk Hause 5 Great End 6 Allen Crags
7 Scoat Fell 8 Kirk Fell 9 Great Gable 10 Green Gable 11 High Stile 12 Glaramara
13 Grasmoor 14 Dale Head 15 Eel Crag 16 Sail 17 Grisedale Pike 18 Causey Pike 19 Lord's Seat
20 Catbells 21 Binsey 22 Ullock Pike 23 Carl Side 24 Skiddaw

95

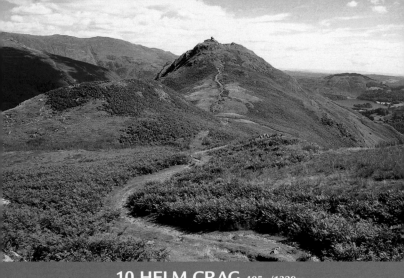

10 HELM CRAG 405M/1329FT

Climb it from	Grasmere 6–9 or Mill Bridge 5
Character	Most cherished and ever-inviting fell above Grasmere and Dunmail Raise
Fell-friendly route	1
Summit grid ref	NY 326 094
Link it with	Gibson Knott
Part of	The Greenburn Horseshoe

This crag is the landmark that defines the Vale of Grasmere. Although the greater bulk of surrounding fells may more regularly lose their heads in cloud, it is this modest height that is known as the cloud-capped ('helmeted') hill. And it's not surprising that it's so well known. People have travelled over Dunmail Raise – the main north–south road through the wild fells of Cumbria – for countless centuries, with all eyes turning in recognition to this one knobbly fell, its iconic summit rocks nicknamed both as an emblem of peace (the Lion and the Lamb), and also of war (the Howitzer).

At a casual glance the fell appears isolated, but fellwalkers know its connection to the delightful roller-coaster ridge running over Gibson Knott to

↑ *Helm Crag from the Gibson Knott ridge*

Calf Crag, ending at the saddle at the very top of Far Easedale. A fine stand-alone objective, too, on a short winter's day or in slower company, its wide views from the heart of the central Lakes are worth the scramble – whether you get right to the top of the rocks or not!

Two of these routes lead up from the popular valley of Easedale (1–2), while the third (3) nips cheekily up from the north in not much more than a mile.

Ascent from Grasmere 6–9

Direct →2.5km/1½ miles ↑340m/1115ft ⏱1hr 30min

Two popular ascents begin from Grasmere village via Easedale Road and make a natural loop.

Follow either Easedale Road or the adjacent fenced path beside the hay meadow to cross Goody Bridge. Now enter Easedale. Beyond Oak Lodge the road leads via a gate through a meadow, and becomes confined once more at Little Parrock. Facing the lane approach to Brimmer Head Farm keep right, signposted 'Far Easedale & Helm Crag'. A cobbled path rises, by

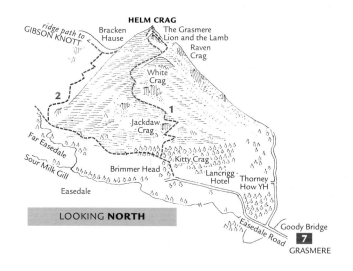

a large dilapidated house, to a metal gate. Note the private walkway (open to the public) signed right to Lancrigg. Known as the 'Poet's Walk' this leads through pleasant woodland to the Lancrigg Hotel – where scrumptious teas are served! From the metal gate two routes diverge.

1 Trend right, through the short lane flanked by woodland, taking the waymarked path which climbs via zig-zags directly ahead above an old quarry. (Older guides and maps show a path slanting right but this one has been rested.) Time, toil and no little funds went into engineering a 'popular' path up the fell. This path is in fact a better route than the old way and enjoys superb views into Far Easedale. It ascends over bare rock at one point before switching right on turf to a saddle. Head north up the ridge and scramble over the southernmost outcrop en route to the summit – which, for most walkers, will be the base of the summit 'howitzer'.

Immediately to the east an ancient landslipped sub-tier gives scope for a spot of exploration. Even if you feel making it to the very top is not your cup of tea, this rough slope will give you a sense of elation and adventure, as not too many visitors venture away from the ridge proper.

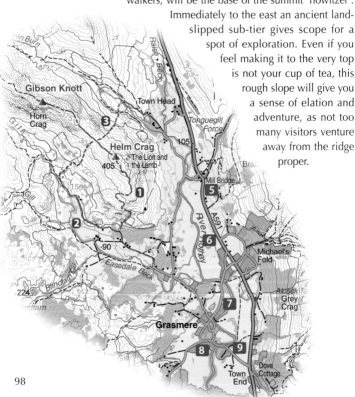

Far Easedale seen during the ascent of Helm Crag

Via Bracken Hause →*3.5km/2¼ miles* ↑*340m/1120ft* ⏲ *1hr 45min*

2 From the metal gate, go left with the bridle-path, again initially flanked by woodland. This track-cum-lane is the age-old pony trail up Far Easedale, destined for Borrowdale via the high watershed of Greenup Edge, now well-trod as part of Alfred Wainwright's Coast to Coast Walk. The rough, tracked lane passes a vernacular barn en route to come alongside **Far Easedale Gill**. As the right-hand wall bears up to the right, follow suit. There is little early evidence of a path but one does materialise, winding up onto a knoll to mount the steep bracken slope. Pass a lone thorn at a spring to reach the saddle of the aptly named Bracken Hause. Go right with the ridge path to the top.

Ascent from Mill Bridge 5

Via Bracken Hause →*2km/1¼ miles* ↑*315m/1035ft* ⏲ *1hr 10min*

This is the nippy route, catching the fell unawares!

3 Follow the minor road down over the Rothay, bearing right by Ghyll Foot to reach the drive access to Helmside. Ascend the metalled lane, via its cattle grids, to the gate beyond **Turn Howe**. Go forward along the level track,

The Grasmere **HELM CRAG**
Lion and the Lamb

Bracken
Hause

Raven
Crag

Goody Bridge

falls

Greenburn Dale

Ghyll Foot

Turn Howe

River Rothay

Helmside

slopes of
STEEL FELL

< GRASMERE

Mill Bridge **5**

Town Head

Raise Beck

A591

Dunmail Raise >

LOOKING **WEST**

passing through a gate, with
Green Burn Beck close down
to the left. Bear left to cross
the wooden footbridge above
the first waterfall. The path
climbs the pasture to cross
the lane, via facing hand-
gates, and climbs directly up
the steep, short turf slope to
Bracken Hause. Turn left with
Route **2** to the summit.

Greenburn Beck

The summit

The ordinary mortal might
feel cheated, having struggled
up the confounded hill only
to find that someone has built
an unassailable fortress on
top, complete with a deep,
dry, stony moat! Steady-
headed scramblers will think

Western aspect of the Howizter, the summit outcrop on Helm Crag

Lines of ascent

nothing of the 7m climb, with either a rib to the south or the northwest groove as their chosen line of ascent. If you don't, console yourself – there is little extra merit in the ultimate view.

Safe descents

Both conventional lines of ascent give secure footing. The route N from Bracken Hause to the footbridge spanning Green Burn (**3**) is steep but mostly free of rock hazard.

Ridge route

Gibson Knott →*1.6km/1 mile* ↓*100m/330ft* ↑*90m/300ft* ⏱*40min*
Descend NW to the saddle depression of Bracken Hause. The ridge path does not always follow the ridge, but keeps a southern bias, though you can tackle the ridge proper with no hazard.

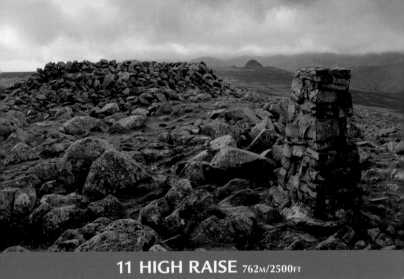

11 HIGH RAISE 762m/2500ft

Climb it from	Stonethwaite **2**, Grasmere **6–9**, Steel End **3** or Stickle Ghyll **17**
Character	High plateau at the very centre of the Cumbrian mountains
Fell-friendly route	7
Summit grid ref	NY 280 095
Link it with	Sergeant Man, Sergeant's Crag, Thunacar Knott or Ullscarf
Part of	The Langdale Pikes

High Raise has a simple symmetry, content with its role as a range-top, scarp-top viewpoint. It lies at the solar plexus of mountain Lakeland, surrounded by more distinctive high points, its plain broad plateau pasture bursting into momentary life only on the brink above Langstrath.

But given half-decent visibility High Raise can make a major panoramic station. The view in the western arc beyond Langstrath and Glaramara features Bowfell, Scafell Pike and Great Gable, with the consistently high switchback skyline of the Helvellyn and Fairfield range forming the eastern horizon. Invariably visitors make this the turning point of their day's walk, a chance to lengthen the stride after a tough pull onto any one of the Langdale Pikes, backtracking to Sergeant Man or Thunacar Knott.

↑ *Summit column and wind shelter on High Raise*

Thanks to its simplicity and its central and superior situation there are any number of radial approaches. Three contrasting routes rise up from Borrowdale, along Greenup Gill (1), Langstrath (3) and the rocky ridge between the two (2). Two climb from Grasmere (4–5), one makes its solitary way up from the southern shore of Thirlmere (6) and the final clutch (7–14) offer myriad ways to make your way through the intricacies of the Langdale Pikes..

Ascent from Stonethwaite 2 *off map N*

Via Greenup Edge →*6.5km/4 miles* ↑*670m/2200ft* ⏱*3hr 45min*

The most efficient route follows the old pony path – its ultimate destination Grasmere.

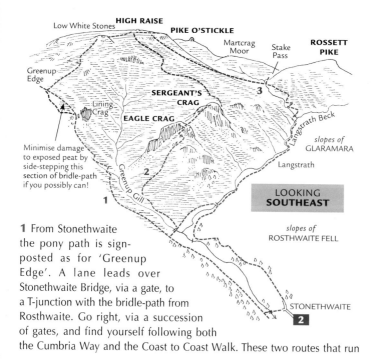

1 From Stonethwaite the pony path is sign-posted as for 'Greenup Edge'. A lane leads over Stonethwaite Bridge, via a gate, to a T-junction with the bridle-path from Rosthwaite. Go right, via a succession of gates, and find yourself following both the Cumbria Way and the Coast to Coast Walk. These two routes that run

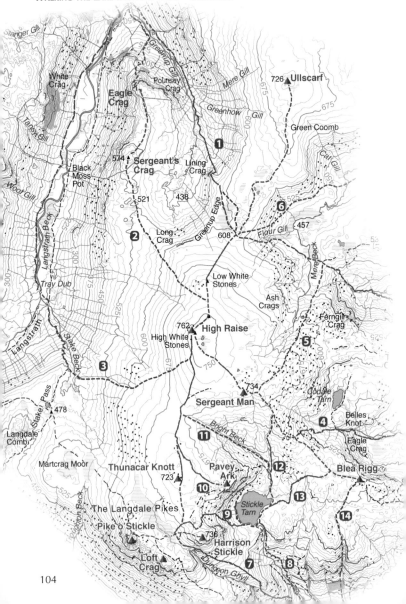

north–south and west–east respectively through the district are, for this brief moment, as one.

Continue up the Greenup Gill valley, with the magnificent shadowed faces of Pounsey and Eagle Crags up to the right and the rock-rimmed edge of **Ullscarf** up to the left. Mounting through the moraine, advance beyond the site of an ancient tarn to clamber up the rock staircase to the left of **Lining Crag**. The summit of the crag is frequently visited as a kind of reward for the effort, and the view down the valley towards now distant Borrowdale is certainly rewarding.

The bridle-path to **Greenup Edge** crosses some particularly bad peat marsh. It is recommended that walkers give it a total miss – both in their own interests and for the welfare of the terrain – by climbing directly up to the ridge-top from Lining Crag (no path), then going right. The line of metal fence posts acts as a guide on the ridge path off Ullscarf, crossing the Greenup Edge depression bound for **Low White Stones**. The climb tackles more peaty ground and a rocky ledge before arrival here. From the stones, the summit is only a short traverse of an easily angled plateau away.

Via Eagle Crag and Sergeant's Crag →6km/3¾ miles ↑685m/2250ft ⏱4hr

This is the adventurer's route, full of drama in the preliminary climb, tailing off on the final pull to the ultimate top.

2 From the hamlet, follow the lane signposted 'Greenup Edge' that leads over the Stonethwaite Beck bridge. After the gate go right, with the gated bridle-track. Cross the footbridge immediately above the confluence of **Greenup Gill** and **Langstrath Beck**. Bear left and cross the fence-stile, taking care to keep on the low side of the flush marsh, with its delicate bog flora. The path brushes through bracken of often monster proportions. Keep parallel with the Greenup Gill fence. Pass through a hand-gate in the down-wall, and while a path continues low beside the wall and gill, continue on the shepherds' path angling gently up the slope to a wall-gap.

At this point the climb proper begins. Keep the partly broken wall to your right, as the path, confirmed by modest, transitory cairns, winds up to a fragile stile at the top of the rising wall hugging the undercliff. Soon a narrow breach in the craggy defences permits a short stair climb. The way beyond suggests two options, but in reality there is but one. (The path leading up left leads to a handsome view of **Pounsey Crag** but there is no safe fellwalking thereafter.) So go immediately right, along the ledge marked with ice-like fragments of quartz, to reach a fine full-height view of Sergeant's Crag. Now switch up, making several similar sharp turns to avoid rock bands, with much heather underfoot, to reach the tilted summit slab of **Eagle Crag**.

Descend south, cross the stile to the right of the wall corner and follow the ridge wall. The path is clear enough, and later it drifts half-right up to the summit of **Sergeant's Crag**. Be mindful that cliffs line the near western slopes.

Continue south from here, crossing the wall-stile, to take a narrow path which weaves through a long marshy saddle and then rises onto drier ground, with less evidence of a path, at the same time losing all sense of a ridge. Keep right of **Long Crag** to reach the skyline at **Low White Stones**, and turn south once more to join Route **1** to the summit.

Via Langstrath →7.5km/4¾ miles ↑670m/2200ft ⏱4hr 15min

A clear route up the less-travelled side of Langstrath to Stake Pass

3 Follow the lane through the hamlet. The gated track passes above the popular camping meadow, latterly passing Alisongrass Hoghouse camping barn.

Stake Beck

As the beck comes closer listen to the roar of Galleny Force down in the tree cover to the left. The track bends right, via a gate, beside the clear cascading waters of **Langstrath Beck**, through a gate to a footbridge.

Follow the west side footpath that climbs over the ladder-stile at Blackmoss, and, at this point, look up to the left for climbers scaling Sergeant's Crag Slabs. Below and above Black Moss Pot the beck takes a wide, shingled, meandering course, with the craggy slopes of Rosthwaite Fall and Glaramara high to the right.

(Alternatively cross the beck to take a closer look at Black Moss Pot, a famous swimming haunt, and cross back at Tray Dub footbridge.) At the end of the valley, cross the bridge and zig-zag up Stake Pass, with some quite amazing water cascades close to the path. As the path eases, branch off left to follow a gill east-southeast. As it is eventually lost make for the skyline and join the path from **Thunacar Knott (7)** going left to the summit.

Ascent from Grasmere 6–9 *off map E*

Via Sergeant Man →*6.5km/4 miles* ↑*670m/2200ft* ⏱*4hr*

The high plateau is hidden from the east by the headwall of Codale Head, which appears to be the culmination of the high ground above Easedale Tarn. Sergeant Man is the crucial link point, enabling walkers to reach the plateau with minimal difficulty, and is best accessed from Eagle Crag (4) or Far Easedale (5).

4 The popular path to Easedale Tarn leaves the Easedale Road via the foot-bridge opposite Oak Lodge, traversing meadows via gates. Much of the way is paved. The path winds up beside Sour Milk Gill, the excited waters churning down frenzied falls. The now-paved parade shows that this walk has long

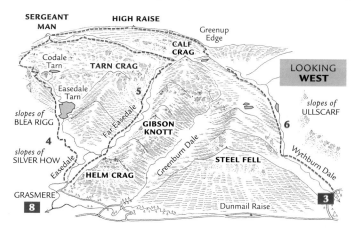

Skiddaw from Codale Head

attracted visitors, for all the drabness of its immediate surroundings. Conical drumlins on either side of **Easedale Tarn** emphasise the glacial origins of this bleak amphitheatre. The top of Tarn Crag looms close right, while Blea Rigg forms the southern sidewall.

The old path continues along the southern side of the tarn and its main feeder-gill, and has several essentially stepped sections beside steep cascades. Up to the right the arresting **Belles Knott** looks like peak worth climbing (scramblers only), but once you get above the falls the knott soon shows itself to be a sham. A side-path bears right, fording the gill, to visit the hanging waters of **Codale Tarn**, with its tiny outflow and picturesque isle set beneath the great slope of Codale Head. Keep with the main path which zig-zags up to a ridge-top path interchange west of Blea Rigg. Turn right and mount the rocky ridge to the northwest for the very first glimpse of the fell-top. Two early path options reunite at the giant slab, and a solitary path continues to ford the outflow of a marsh and then climbs the distinctive summit knoll of **Sergeant Man** beyond. From here, head northwest, passing pools in crossing the open plateau. Skirt the old fence-corner by even larger pools to reach the summit.

5 Leave Broadgate opposite Sam Read's bookshop, along Easedale Road. This leads naturally onto the signposted bridle-path running into **Far Easedale**. After crossing the Stythwaite Steps footbridge keep right, with the one clear path, which has a few rough sections en route to the saddle at the dale head. Turn left here and follow the few forlorn metal stakes – all that remain of a fence that once marked the Cumberland–Westmorland county boundary – to the summit of **Sergeant Man** where turn right to join Route **4** to the summit.

Ascent from Steel End 3 *off map NE*

Via Greenup Edge →*6km/3¾ miles* ↑*680m/2230ft* ⏱*3hr 20min*

In many eyes this is the most dreary route, as it wends up the lonely wastes of Wythburn Dale, avoiding any hint of rocky outcropping.

6 Take the path leading up the north bank of the Wyth Burn from the road bridge opposite the car park. Reach and cross the footbridge underneath Rake Crags, just where the valley begins to constrict, to follow the clear path climbing up the south side of the ravine below Black Crag. The dale reopens becoming progressively more desolate and the beck slothfully winds through a gently curving tarn. Keep on until, just past **The Bog**, you cross Calf Gill to come along the northern side of **Flour Gill** and join the rising pony path which climbs steadily, and eventually steeply, up the head of the valley to reach **Greenup Edge**. Here turn left with great relief and generous views to join the line of Route **1** to the summit. (Alternatively, turn up and left pathlessly off the main track not long after the foot-bridge mid-dale to gain the **Calf Crag** ridge, summit and a wider perspective earlier in your expedition.)

Codale Head and Ash Crags from Wythburn Head

Ascent from Stickle Ghyll 17

No expedition to climb Harrison Stickle, Pavey Ark or even Blea Rigg and Sergeant Man is truly complete without taking in the summit of the plateau. There are a number of braided routes to choose from. Only Route 11 is exclusive to High Raise.

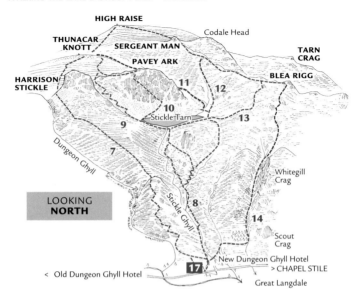

Via Harrison Combe →4km/2½ miles ↑685m/2250ft ⏱3hr

Rising above the dramatic gorge of Dungeon Ghyll this route crosses Harrison Combe to the summit of Thunacar Knott and beyond.

7 Go either directly up the bridle-path from the hotel or ascend from Stickle Ghyll car park information shelter. The paths meet up by the fence-gap. Here this route leads off left from the paved path, rises to a hand-gate and turns right, passing a seat to a stile. Keep the wall on your right, and do not ford **Dungeon Ghyll**. The well-marked path bears left mounting the steep slope in steady stages. Much of it has been re-engineered to cope with the inevitable heavy foot traffic. Climbing up to the saddle behind Pike How, the path proceeds across the open pasture aiming west-northwest for the high shoulder above the deep upper gorge of Dungeon Ghyll. Take your time and watch your footing, as there is loose ground to negotiate. On entering Harrison Combe come to the path junction above the peat-hopping stepping-stones.

From here curve round to the right (northeast), skirting the rock tor and then turn due north to climb pathless towards the southern cairn which marks the summit of **Thunacar Knott** and the start of an easy northerly stride down to join the ridge path from **Pavey Ark**, cross the depression at the head of **Bright Beck** and rise gently to the summit.

Via Stickle Tarn →4km/2½ miles ↑685m/2250ft ⏱3hr 10min

Climb Stickle Ghyll by any one of three clear paths and then choose from five onward lines of approach to High Raise. Route 9 climbs the scree to skirt Harrison Stickle, Route 10 takes the classic climbers' route up the face of Pavey Ark while Routes 11, 12 and 13 make gentler, more oblique journeys to the summit.

8 Follow Route **7** and fork off right on the paved path at the fence-gap to climb **Stickle Ghyll**. Even here there are three lines. The zig-zag path which draws under Tarn Crag is better than the unflinching gill path, while the green trod climbing on from the zig-zag is an altogether quieter option still.

From the shores of **Stickle Tarn** five routes spring.

9 The eastern approach to **Harrison Stickle** climbs the scree slope. Work up the slope to the right of the buttresses. As the contouring path from **Pavey Ark** joins, go straight up onto the saddle. Keep right, rounding a tor to cross the shoulder of **Thunacar Knott**, now upon the ridge path **7**.

10 Jack's Rake is the route that all true mountaineers take as their royal route to High Raise. Take the path by the west shore of the tarn, climbing the scree slope from the northwest edge of the tarn via a prominent memorial cairn inscribed 'S.W.S. 1900'. There are five distinct stages to the climb. There are several places to take a breath, at an ash tree and a patch of thistles. The ascent features a squeeze behind a fallen splinter of rock (The Gun) and concludes above Great Gully, dipping momentarily, then scrambling up rock slabs to the wall end above a projecting rock. The instinct to climb, so well developed by now, means that you naturally find a scrambly way to the top of **Pavey Ark**, thereafter taking the clear path leading off west and curving north-west to the head of **Bright Beck** to fall into step with Route **7**.

Either **11** follow **Bright Beck** from the head of the tarn, through its upper ravine to the broad depression north of **Thunacar Knott** and there join Route

7, or **12** ford **Bright Beck**, making (due north) to join the path to High Raise (**4**) via the rounded summit of **Sergeant Man**.

13 Take the path that runs along the southern shore of the tarn from the outflow east to meet an old shepherds' path coming up from the New Dungeon Ghyll. A clear, occasionally cairned path leads north and east towards **Blea Rigg**. Climb left onto the ridge bound for **Sergeant Man** and the plateau beyond, to meet Route **4**.

Via Blea Rigg →4km/2½ miles ↑685m/2250ft ⏱3hr 10min

An exciting variant, side-stepping Stickle Tarn.

14 Pass up by the hotel to the gate, slant right in the triangular enclosure and cross the footbridge. The path rises above Millbeck Farm via a hand-gate on a path between a wall and a gill. Go through the kissing-gate on the right after 100m, keep the wall to the right and pass through the foot of a larch plantation to cross a low wall into the bouldery ravine. The combined effects of path and gill erosion ensure a loose, clambering way. Above the tree trend to the left for bigger boulder steps and more secure footing. Much of the gill-bed is dry, with subterranean flow. The natural exit draws into a short, tight gully to the right, requiring a spot of mild scrambling. Ignore the gill-head itself. The summit of **Blea Rigg** beckons across undulating slopes of outcropping. While there is no evident path, a route is easily concocted.

From here to **Sergeant Man** the occasional cairn indicates a surprisingly modest ridge trail. Just short of the path interchange admire the rock basin where cairns now abound. From here the ridge narrows, with rocky outcrops, including one notable tilted slab. The path forks, then reunites on the steady climb to the outflow of the marsh west of **Codale Head**. The summit is swiftly attained on the popular and worn final path. Here join the last segment of Route **4** to reach your destination.

The summit

This is aptly called High White Stones. Among the pale surface rocks sits a capacious wind-shelter, within which half a dozen may huddle when all about is torrid and foul, and a stone-built Ordnance Survey pillar to lean against when fortune brings a balmy sun. This is a place of congregation and expansive scenic pleasure. While some walkers, having gained their bearings, speed on to craggier attractions elsewhere, those who adore just being on top of the world dally long, soaking up this the purest of Lakeland fellscapes, with Glaramara centre stage setting the inspirational tone across the obscured depths of Langstrath. In appearance the fell-top has more in common with the Far Eastern Fells, being an almost pancake-flat pasture where sheep wander at will.

Safe descents

The remote situation carries a price. Innocuous as the broad, peaty-pastured top appears to be, do not be tempted to beeline north as Long Crag is a nasty trap. The surest recourse is to Greenup Edge, joining the well-marked range-crossing pony path. Head NNE for 600m to High White Stones, then NNE (**1**) down to the damp depression. For Grasmere turn right, E, descending initially beside Flour Gill as you cross the rough slope at the head of Wythburn Dale, then fording Mere Beck and rising to the low saddle at the very top of Far Easedale. The path (**5**) runs securely down this wild dale via the Stythwaite Steps footbridge. For Borrowdale, go left NNW (**1**), being watchful to keep to the right at Lining Crag. After descending a gully, the path runs down the Greenup Gill valley bound for Stonethwaite, 5km away, and Rosthwaite, 6km.

Ridge pool with High White Stones in the background

High Raise from Harrison Stickle

The Stake Pass route (**3**) is certainly a safe line for either Borrowdale or Great Langdale, but it almost doubles any journey, and on such grounds should be a last recourse. It is best reached (no path) from the depression at the head of Bright Beck. Southbound routes engage in more tricky terrain, though remember that Sergeant Man is the key for Easedale (**4**), as is Thunacar Knott for Langdale, via Harrison Combe and the Pike How route (**7**) leading down from the head of Dungeon Ghyll.

Ridge routes

Sergeant Man →*0.8km/½ mile* ↓*30m/100ft* ↑*10m/35ft* ⊕*20min*
Walk SSE passing the shallow pools and peaty ground to join the vestige of the metal fence. The summit comes into view as the plateau unfolds.

Sergeant's Crag →*2.4km/1½ miles* ↓*195m/640ft* ↑*10m/30ft* ⊕*40min*
Advance to Low White Stones, and from here leave the plateau WNW on a rough, pathless descent, mindful that Long Crag lurks to the northwest. There is little evidence of a ridge until the reedy depression at the foot of the slope is reached. Then one materialises, as too now does a path, leading to the stile in the summit-embracing wall.

Thunacar Knott →*1.6km/1 mile* ↓*85m/280ft* ↑*50m/160ft* ⊕*30min*
The main path leads S, gently declining to a broad depression. As the first rocks are encountered along the easy rise, bear off right from the main trail. Otherwise the path makes for Pavey Ark.

Ullscarf →*4km/2½ miles* ↓*155m/510ft* ↑*120m/390ft* ⊕*1hr*
Head NNE for 600m to Low White Stones, then descend NNE to Greenup Edge. Go straight on accompanying the line of metal stakes. Sweep past at least one notable pool before rising onto the drier ridge. Aim north with only the merest of stumps (watch you don't stumble on them) for guides to the solitary summit cairn.

12 LINGMOOR FELL 470M/1542FT

Climb it from	Elterwater **16**, Little Langdale **19**, Blea Tarn **20** or Stickle Ghyll **17**
Character	A superlative ridge from which to admire the scenic qualities of Great and Little Langdale
Fell-friendly route	1
Summit grid ref	NY 303 046

Sitting right in the middle of all the scenic action, with Great and Little Langdale to north and south, and three lakes to east, west and south – Elter Water, Blea Tarn and Little Langdale Tarn – how could anyone not adore this little fell? It even cradles its own tiny sheet of water high among the rank heather that gave it its name. Wooded to the north and east, rugged to the south and west, and sprinkled with slate workings, the fell has much to merit a casual exploration.

As the east–west ridge tapers to the west it throws up the sturdy boss of Side Pike. It's a stout individualist, a fell in miniature and an excellent first-evening climb for a fellwalking holiday. Its east-facing crags effectively shut off the ridge, forcing walkers onto a narrow ledge beneath the southeast face, and the summit provides a peerless view of a famous valley-head, featuring the Langdale Pikes,

↑ West along the ridge to Side Pike (photo: Maggie Allan) 115

Mickleden, Bowfell and the handsome heights about Oxendale – Crinkle Crags, Pike o'Blisco and Kettle Crag. Great Langdale bends around its northern spur and on the tip of this ridge is a blunt pinnacle, Oak How Needle.

Lines of ascent from all around the compass are offered here so you can create your own personal circuit from any given starting point.

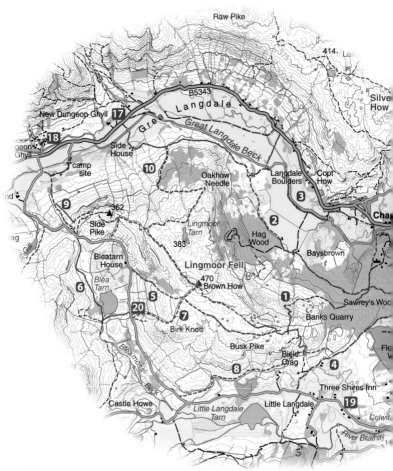

LOOKING **SOUTHWEST**

LINGMOOR FELL

Oakhow Needle

Wrynose Pass

4

1

LITTLE LANGDALE

19

2

GREAT LANGDALE

3

CHAPEL STILE

Burlington Slate

Wainwrights' Inn

The Langdale Estate

slopes of SILVER HOW

16

ELTERWATER

Colwith

Elter Water

Ascent from Elterwater 16

Via Baysbrown Wood →*3.2km/2 miles* ↑*405m/1330ft*
🕐*2hr 25min*

*The classic route up from Elterwater can be started in two dif-
ferent ways. If you're not interested in seeing the stone works,
use the second one described here.*

1 Cross the road bridge with a choice of two routes. For the first,
bear right, branching right from the quarry access roadway, guided
by signs, after taking a back view of the **Langdale Estate** holiday
accommodation and enjoy a delightful wooded stroll near the River
Brathay. Ignoring, if you can, the footbridge to **Wainwrights' Inn**, continue upstream. The route is promptly drawn up a corridor path away from the

river. Rising beneath slate tip, much of it naturalised by birch, continue to the busy entrance to **Burlington's** stone works, a store and processing plant for decorative architectural slate. Pass a weighbridge and showroom that might tempt you to inspect the stylish product. The path crosses into a quiet lane leading up to an open metalled road, still within the woods. (Alternatively this point can reached from the village by following the Colwith road south from Bridge End, passing Elterwater Hostel. Where the road forks, go right by Elterwater Hall. This deteriorates into a track. At this point keep to the metalled road which bears right by Ullet Nest Cottage. Join the route from Burlington Slate at the path intersection.)

Bear off the metalled road (bound for Baysbrown Farm). Follow the track southwest, rising further into Baysbrown Wood. This old track reaches a gate by the abandoned **Banks Quarry**. Continue curving with a gill re-entrant, then, level with a solitary yew, take leave of the old quarry track on a path winding up to a ladder-stile in the ridge-top wall. Go up right, inspecting the ruin at the scarp edge above Lingmoor Quarry. Follow the ridge path running close to the wall. As **Brown How** swells ahead the wall is replaced by a fence and the path veers half-left before taking on the broken ground to reach the fence-stile and the summit, immediately above the fence junction.

Great Langdale valley paths

Great Langdale can be enjoyed as much from valley level as from on high. There are two principal footpaths, each useful as a means of avoiding traffic on the congested valley road, particularly to be coveted when devising a circular walk incorporating the ridge-top path.

From Eltermere Hotel to Old Dungeon Ghyll 18 →6km/3¾ miles
↑290m/950ft ◷1hr 25min

2 The better of these paths hugs the northern base of the fell via **Baysbrown Farm** and is approached along the open road through Baysbrown Wood which becomes a walled lane to the farm. Pass on via a gate, where it branches off right, from the old Spoutcrag Quarry track. Notice the odd road-sign directing to 'Great Langdale'! Approaching Oak How, fork left, via the old walled lane, leading via a gate beneath the steep northern spur of **Oakhow Needle**. After a further hand-gate, descend a pasture to **Side House**. A permissive path has been created, continuing (via ladder-stiles) across the damp pasture slopes to slip through the Langdale camp site.

From Wainwrights' Inn to New Dungeon Ghyll 17 → 3.6km/2¼ miles ↑25m/80ft ⏱1hr

3 A pleasant alternative keeps closer to **Great Langdale Beck**, a route adopted in part by the Cumbria Way. In effect this begins from Wainwrights' Inn and follows a lane behind the school, then bears down to a bridge over the beck. The track continues west either by Oak How, or a footbridge right onto the valley road. Going left after 100m, enter a bridle-lane which leads, rather neatly, directly to the NP Langdale/NT Stickle Ghyll car parks... and attendant hostelries.

Ascent from Little Langdale 19

If you can tear yourself away from the pub, this approach is straightforward and full of interest.

Via Bield Crag → 2.7km/1¾ miles ↑365m/1200ft ⏱1hr 25min

4 From the vicinity of the **Three Shires Inn** follow the road steeply up past the unusual first-floor church and leave it to the right on the lane to Dale End Farm. Beyond the farm take a footpath signed left, leaving the lane, via a ladder-stile. Two further decrepit specimens are crossed before the path turns up a combe, zig-zagging in a measured progress. The ladder-stile in the wall up to the right only gives access to the ridge-end top. A prominent cairn on **Bield Crag** up to the left may be reached by a lateral path under the edge, beginning before the zig-zagging path reaches the easier gradient. The main path sweeps up the grassy ridge, meeting up with the path from **Banks Quarry** (**1**). Either opt to follow the ridge, or do a spot of exploration (marked in green on the map). An intermittent path branches half-left, running through an area of small slate tips and ruined huts, the remnants of a cottage industry manufacturing roof slates: the slate is of excellent quality and possesses a lovely tone. The path levels and wanders along a lateral valley before meeting the path climbing from **Bleatarn House** at a stile in a marsh. Switch sharp right by the fence to the fragile stile at the fence junction and thus the summit cairn.

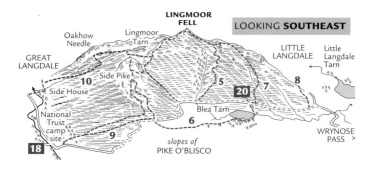

Ascent from Blea Tarn 20

From here three routes naturally suggest themselves.

Via Bleatarn House →2km/1¼ miles ↑260m/850ft ⏱1hr 10min

A straightforward ascent up a clear grassy path

5 Embark from the part-open road 400m north of the car park, and short of **Bleatarn House**, referred to as 'The Solitary' by Wordsworth. A clear grassy path climbs to a wall gap, then winds up the steep slope with larch engulfing a re-entrant close to the left. The path reaches a stile in a fence at the head of this gully. The wet ground is quickly left behind on the climb beside the fence to the summit.

Blea Tarn

Via Blea Tarn and Side Pike →3.2km/2 miles ↑270m/890ft ⏱1hr 45min

The scenic way to tackle the west ridge

6 Follow the path that runs from the hand-gate directly opposite the car park entrance. It saunters down to a kissing-gate and subsequent footbridge over the outflow of **Blea Tarn**. The luxuriant surroundings attract people and wildlife in almost equal measure. On a recent visit a peregrine falcon was audibly making its presence felt from the outcrop directly above the plantation. Rhododendrons love this place too. Across the lapping waters of the tarn attention is grabbed by Side Pike and the backing Langdale Pikes: a composition to tempt the shyest camera from the rucksack.

The squeeze on Side Pike

Keeping the lake in sight, head north to exit via a further hand-gate. The path traverses to a kissing-gate in a wall, reaching the road summit beside a cattle grid. Climb the ladder-stile opposite and, passing the stone seat, ascend, either rounding the slope to the right, scrambling up from the top of the wall ahead, or better still slant half-left to follow the regular path mounting more comfortably up to the ridge wall. The ridge path negotiates several small outcrops rising in harmony with the broken ridge wall to the summit cairn on **Side Pike**. A few paces further and the ground falls precipitously! There is absolutely no scope to continue directly up the ridge, unless you are equipped for abseiling!

Backtrack west, keeping a smart eye out for the narrow trod which sneaks left onto a shelf below the southern cliff. The shelf path ends at a firm flake, which creates a 'squeeze' which will cause many walkers to question their chances of escape. (You could try putting your rucksack through first!) The subsequent path dips to a stile crossing a fence, here joining the path serving the less adventurous, rising direct from the road. The path proceeds with

A majestic view along the ridge to Langdale (photo: Ron Kenyon)

the undulating ridge wall climbing to cross a stile. A faint path bears left at this point. This is the natural means of reaching **Lingmoor Tarn**, a detour the solitary wanderer will savour. The vicinity of the tarn is pathless and damp. Simply rejoin the ridge up the rough heather slopes. The ridge path scrambles up a rock-step, hugging the well-made wall, curving onto a prominent knoll topped with a cairn. Henceforward the wall is bettered by a straggling fence leading to the summit.

Via Birk Knott →*2km/1¼ miles* ↑*270m/890ft* ⏱*1hr 10min*

The most direct ascent

7 Climb straight up from the south side of the cattle grid almost due east onto **Birk Knott**, following the skyline wall north-northeast to **Brown How** and the summit.

Link route from Blea Tarn Road to Bield Crag →*1.6km/1 mile* ↑*140m/460ft* ⏱*25min*

A lovely path, which comes into its own when creating a circular outing with a southern bias, follows the intake wall off the open road, south of the car park.

8 Find the barrier – slung across a green track on the left. Follow this track east as it becomes a path in curving into a re-entrant. Ford the gill, keeping above the intake wall, climbing more steeply after High Bield to gain a superb view south across Little Langdale Tarn to Wetherlam and meet up with the zig-zagging path beneath **Bield Crag**.

Ascent from Stickle Ghyll 17

Via Side Pike →*3.2km/2 miles* ↑*380m/1250ft* ⏱*1hr 40min*

Follow clear paths to the summit of Side Pike and the west ridge.

9 Follow the valley road south from the bus stop. Join a footpath which leaves the road left, via the camp site wood, and rise via kissing-gates onto the pasture, with a wall right. The path has two branches. The left option brings you to the base of the Side Pike ridge, with a clear path climbing to the ridge wall and thus to the summit cairn on **Side Pike** to join Route **6**.

Via Oakhow Needle →*3.2km/2 miles* ↑*380m/1250ft* ⏱*1hr 25min*

A wanderer's route, with a long pathless section on the way

10 Cross the beck from the car park and follow the path leading east from **Side House**, rising to a hand-gate. Bear up right, keeping the wall close right. Don't be put off by the juniper. A way can be won through the dense foliage via an outcrop. Where the wall dips right, take the opportunity to climb straight on up the rigg. As the ground eases traverse left over a rough pathless fellside to locate the blunt **Oakhow Needle** but don't get too close as a rough scree gully intervenes. Climb back up the ridge to find the outflow of **Lingmoor Tarn**, where a path, largely holding a contouring line, wanders west to meet the ridge path by the wall at the stile below the inclined slab. Turn left with Route **6** to the summit.

The summit

The final rise above the fence junction is crowned with a modest cairn among ragged heather. The view is the thing, and very fine it is too – the Langdale

The summit

Pikes in all their majesty, the prominent stack of Pike o'Stickle, Loft Crag surmounting Gimmer Crag, Harrison Stickle above the secretive ravine of Dungeon Ghyll, Stickle Beck falling in fuming steps from the cragface of Pavey Ark. Elsewhere the bounty is no less exciting – westward Bowfell, Crinkle Crags and to the south the Coniston fells, all in startling contrast with the rolling, richly wooded country running east towards Windermere.

Safe descents

The ridge wall-cum-fence offers all the security you require in time of need. W (**6**) to the saddle before Side Pike, keep left to reach the Bleatarn road and turn right for the Old Dungeon Ghyll. E descend steadily. For Elterwater find the ladder-stile after the quarry-edge ruin (**1**). For Little Langdale follow the path which winds down the ensuing combe and cross three ladder-stiles to reach the lane above Dale End Farm (**4**). Go SW (**7**) for the quickest route to a road, follow the fence down to a stile in a wet hollow. The path bears half-left. Avoiding the larch-filled gill, descend to the open road south of Bleatarn House.

13 LITTLE STAND 739M/2426FT

Climb it from	Cockley Beck Bridge **24**
Character	Shy ridge-end peppered with pools and rocks
Summit grid ref	NY 250 034
Link it with	Crinkle Crags

Judgment has traditionally been reserved as to whether Little Stand is a stand-alone fell, or just a minor ridge adjunct of its more illustrious and elevated ridge partner, Crinkle Crags. Orientated towards the Duddon Valley rather than Great Langdale, it is, however, clearly a prominent and distinct headland – a fell of standing, even – with a definite summit and a highly characterful plateau to explore before the northern run of the ridge leads to the impressive haystack upthrust of the fifth crinkle of Crinkle Crags.

Travellers viewing the fell from Cockley Beck Bridge will see no comfortable ridge sweeping to the sky, but the direct rough ascent up from the south (1) causes little difficulty. Curiously, the Ordnance Survey maps mark a path streaking up the fell from the dale bottom, but only the bridleway further west has any credibility. From the southernmost limit of the summit ridge, the broad view of the delectable Duddon Valley, above the ancient Roman causeway between Hard Knott and Wrynose, is well worth the climb.

↑ *Little Stand from Cockley Beck* 125

The other ascent offered here (2) takes a long line north beside mossy Mosedale before climbing pathless over Stonesty Pike to the summit ridge.

Ascent from Cockley Beck Bridge 24

Viewed from the walk's start the fell seems a quite rotten broken slope ameliorated by the inviting skyline which simply bristles with rock. With the swirl of a furtive cloud it is at times reminiscent of a remote Munro. Nonetheless, the direct approach (Route 1), for the free-thinking independent fell-traveller, has a measure of pleasure. Route 2 is more laborious but would make a good return path.

Direct via Gaitsgill Close →2km/1¼ miles ↑520m/1710ft ⊕1hr 10min
1 Ford **Mosedale Beck** just west of Cockley Beck Bridge to a gate/stile (footpath sign). After 50m angle quarter-left across damp ground to find a track rising up the bracken bank to the left of another gill. This is all damp stuff, but it brings you to a wall gap and, a little beyond, a stile in the wire fence.

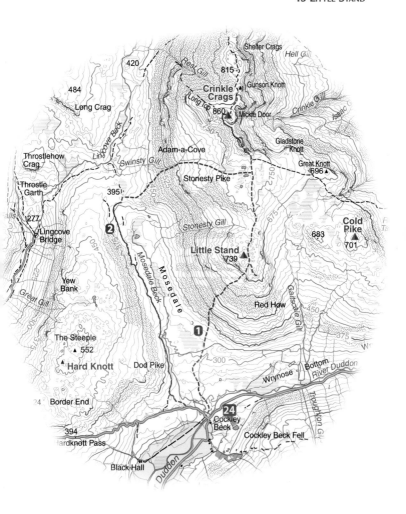

Now set a course up the rough slope in the Gaitscale Close enclosure. There is no obvious path up among the boulders, though as you emerge onto the upper pasture shelf as if by magic a path materialises, drawing you up to the apparent saddle between prominent skyline outcrops. Gaining the ridge path, an initial right turn reveals the view from the ridge-end, while the summit cairn lies up to the left, off the more tangible path.

Via Mosedale →*5km/3 miles* ↑*560m/1840ft* ⏱*2hr*
2 The Mosedale bridleway is signed off the open **Hardknott Pass** road, a short distance west of Cockley Beck Bridge. This leads off purposefully and with some early pitching, keeping largely to the **Hard Knott** fell slope. Go immediately right along the dale head moraine ridge-top, accompanying the fence up the grass slope to **Adam-a-Cove** and the cluster of ridge-top tarns, most of which are skirted on the north side to reach the ridge path. Turn right, south, to **Little Stand**.

The summit

The cairn rests on outcrops just to the west of the ridge path. Beneath it to the west are lovely pools, while a large tarn sits in the hollow to the east cradled by a great slab. The view is fully worthy of the effort but it's better to venture to the southernmost limit of the ridge to appraise the Duddon Valley.

Wetherlam from the south top

Safe descents

The fell-top is girdled with outcrops making a truly comfortable descent extremely unlikely. Stonesty Gill leads to the worst of the Mosedale marsh, and beware that bracken swathes lower Gaitscale Gill, making that equally unattractive in high summer. The best advice is to reserve any visit for a clear dry day and be prepared to backtrack to Adam-a-cove in descent to side-step the worst of Mosedale's dampness.

The summit cairn

Ridge Route

Crinkle Crags →2km/1¼ miles ↓20m/70ft ↑140m/460ft ⊕1hr 25min
The ridge path leads precisely due N and even the novice will find no problem in determining where the fifth crinkle might be expected – a simple
scramble. Cross into the gap to tackle the Bad Step, or, better, angle up left on
a secure path to the saddle on the Long Top ridge west of the summit.

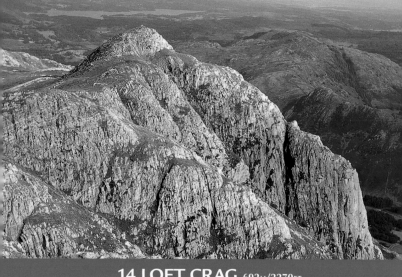

14 LOFT CRAG 692M/2270FT

Climb it from	Stickle Ghyll **17** or Old Dungeon Ghyll **18**
Character	Easily reached summit above an impressive crag
Fell-friendly route	1
Summit grid ref	NY 277 071
Link it with	Harrison Stickle or Pike o'Stickle
Part of	The Langdale Pikes

To rock climbers Loft Crag is merely the attic floor of Gimmer Crag, a much-revered cliff. To fellwalkers it is the central component of the southern group of the Langdale Pikes, sitting between Harrison Stickle and Pike o'Stickle. To its east, underling top, Thorn Crag, cramps the upper ravine of Dungeon Ghyll but does not quite have the stature to be counted a member of this iconic group.

The clearest view of Loft Crag, and the tiers of rock spilling down its southern flank towards Mickleden, is from the summit of Pike o'Stickle. The short northern slope runs down behind, with much less drama, to the marshy hollow of Harrison Combe. Returning the favour, the top of Loft Crag is the most thrilling spot from which to admire Pike o'Stickle, and also masterly Bowfell and a great sweep of Great Langdale.

↑ *Loft Crag from Pike o'Stickle*

But you cannot know the fell thoroughly by sticking to the ridge-top. For a spot of exploration follow the climbers' traverse off the Mark Gate path to admire Gimmer Crag from below then clamber up beside the easternmost gully onto the tiny col on the summit ridge where the right-hand gullies (known to climbers as Junipal and Southeastern) converge.

A couple of lines up from the bottom of Langdale are described here, with some exciting variants for happy scramblers and fellwanderers.

Ascent from Stickle Ghyll 17

Routes spring from both of the two Dungeon Ghyll Hotels.

Via Mark Gate →*2.5km/1½ miles* ↑*600m/1970ft* ⏲*1hr 20min*

The most secure path, known as Mark Gate, has received a tremendous amount of pitching and paving – enough to make you feel you are climbing a castle rampart rather than a wild fell. Confident scramblers could opt to take a closer look at the Ghyll (Route 2) on the way up, and Gimmer Crag (Route 3) for the last stretch of the ascent.

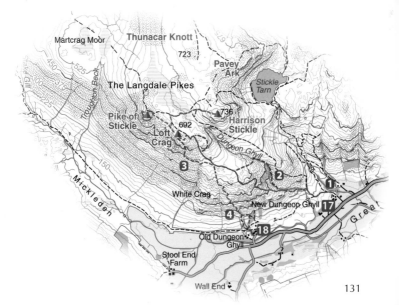

1 Walk up behind the **New Dungeon Ghyll**. Keep left as you rise to a hand-gate, turn right past the seat and clamber over the stile. Turn left, dipping to ford **Dungeon Ghyll's** rough boulder bed. Now that you are properly upon **Mark Gate**, respect those sections shut off to nurture turf recovery. As the path veers from the wall you could slip into the ravine to squint into the dark recesses of Dungeon Ghyll Force – there is no way through at this point. Backtrack and follow the path winding uphill.

At the next relaxation in the ravine, directly upstream of the 'dungeon' section, either keep with the primary path or take the opportunity to enter the ravine proper (**2**). Mark Gate is the unambiguous high way to the top, winding steeply above the lower tier of buttresses and pell-mell of outcrops that bear down on the Old Dungeon Ghyll Hotel. Arriving on the moor, the path advances west-northwest to a sheepfold and cairn, where outcropping resumes. From the cairn the climbers' traverse to the famous buttresses of Gimmer Crag may be pursued (**3**). From this point on the slope steepens once more, bringing further paving leading either directly onto the saddle overlooking Harrison Combe or, after the first outcrop, bearing up right onto

Old Dungeon Ghyll Hotel overlooked by Raven Crag

Thorn Crag and down again. If you choose to detour this way enjoy its fine view of Harrison Crag across the gulf of the upper gorge of Dungeon Ghyll.

When the paths reunite contour, then bear up left, on a loose, stony-bedded path to access the summit.

2 The middle section of **Dungeon Ghyll** runs so deep into the breast of the Pikes that as you branch off the path to enter it you feel you are venturing beyond the limits of reason to end in some hidden kingdom of doom. Do so cautiously and beware of the tree roots. Scramble over the mid-gill rocks to follow the right bank up to the first mare's-tail waterfall. Scramble dexterously up the right-hand outcrop. The scenery is superb. Keep to the right bank until forced onto the left side, then climb up through the large boulders to reach the upper fall. A thunderous scene awaits: water crashing into a pool before finally spilling to the gill floor. The exit is the unlikely looking gully to the left, and a scramble leads onto the open fell pasture to join Mark Gate (**1**) – and return to the kingdom of light!

3 At the cairn before Thorn Crag fork left to **Gimmer Crag**. While confident climbers may tackle the Southeastern Gully, those less adept should divert off the path earlier and aim up to the much shorter easternmost gully. Even this has a 3m chockstone 'Bad Step', side-stepped up easily handled rocks on the right-hand side. Once above simply follow the grassy ledge above the

Pike o' Stickle from the top of Junipal Gully

Northwestern Gully to join the ridge west of the summit and walk back right.

Alternatively, having completed the full scramble, take the opportunity to visit the thrilling col at the top of Gimmer Crag. Look for, then follow, the short, tilted rock-and-grass rake to the left, switching precisely at its top. Zig-zag through the early outcropping and contour along a ledge on the right to arrive at the tiny col immediately above the plummeting Junipal Gully. From here Pike o'Stickle seems to soar! Looking back up the fellside, a solid mass of banded rock suggests you are crag-bound, and you would be… but for the knowledge of your approach! Before you retreat, gaze behind you down Southeastern Gully.

Ascent from Old Dungeon Ghyll 18

The path of this route, over a range of terrain, is never in doubt.

Direct →2.5km/1½ miles ↑580m/1900ft ◷1hr 15min

4 From the Old Dungeon Ghyll car park follow the path up behind the hotel, via a gate. Cross directly over the bridleway to the ladder-stile. Winding up the light plantation, bear left just as the flight of steps begins – these are for the express use of rock climbers accessing Middlefell Buttress and Raven Crag. Ford the tiny gill to reach a stile in the fence at the top of the wall. The path tackles the scree slope, and progressively firmer footing is found through the mild outcropping and light bracken as it climbs to an obvious fork. The climbers' path, rather oddly, chooses to follow the initially inviting ledge path on the left. The path falls foul of steep ground as a gill re-entrant is neared, causing it to climb steeply before slanting left beneath the upper fall, angling up towards Gimmer Crag. The immeasurably better route is straight up, on an easy grassy slope, directly to the cairn, where the climbers' traverse leaves Mark Gate. Join Route **1** or Route **3** to reach the summit.

The summit

This is an ideal summit in many respects – quite small, yet with ample room for a party to sit and relish the view. Great Langdale is especially prominent, with Mickleden far below, and Bowfell forming the dark majestic backdrop. The stuff of fellwalking dreams.

Safe descents

For all the ferocity of tiered crags directly beneath their feet the walker has a sure recourse in Mark Gate (**1**). Leave the summit on the path heading SE. Bear left down the stony trail, and note that at the foot of this short ramp the stones are at their loosest. Join the contouring path below the northern slope of the summit. Go right, and the evident cairned path soon begins its paved descent – destination the New Dungeon Ghyll.

Ridge routes

Harrison Stickle →0.4km/¼ mile ↓60m/200ft ↑105m/345ft ⏱25min
To split hairs, this is not strictly a ridge route – rather these are two summits with a natural harmony. You climb one… you want to climb the other! Go NW off the summit ridge to join the worn trail from Pike o'Stickle, then go right to cross the large boulders in the peaty hollow of Harrison Combe, from where two paths lead to the summit. The direct route encounters an easy rock-step, whilst the left-hand route sweeps up and round to approach from the northwest over easy ground every step of the way.

Pike o'Stickle →0.4km/¼ mile ↓25m/80ft ↑60m/200ft ⏱20min
Leave the summit to the NW, following the undulating ridge to the top of South Scree. From here there are at least four lines of scrambly ascent up the massive summit cone – how many can you discover.

15 LOUGHRIGG FELL 335M/1099FT

Climb it from	Clappersgate **13**, Ambleside **12**, Tarn Foot **14**, Pelter Bridge **11**, White Moss **10** or High Close **15**
Character	A fellwanderer's delight, with a labyrinth of winding ways to the top
Fell-friendly route	11
Summit grid ref	NY 347 051

At the point where the rivers Rothay and Brathay meet to flow into Windermere, the Central Fells are born in the irregular form of Loughrigg Fell. The fell climbs above Clappersgate and the site of Galava Roman Fort and rises onto Todd Crag, a lowly but strategic viewpoint for the great lake. Its undulating mass of bracken-clad fell and pasture trends northwest while a further ridge rises from Rydal village to run southwestward over Lanty Scar. The two converge at a damp amphitheatre before mounting confidently over Ivy Crag to the triple-top summit.

Well endowed with paths at every level the fell is a parade for all manner of walkers. By Rydal Water and Grasmere the fell provides a near perfect expression of the picturesque in the promenade of Loughrigg Terrace. The higher portions of the fell have wilder ground, harbouring pools and undulations, where, were it not for the bracken, you might wander at will enjoying the exceptionally lovely

↑ *Loughrigg Fell beyond Red Bank from Silver How*

outlooks. The fell also has one great work of audacious quarrying, Loughrigg Cavern (sometimes called Rydal Cave) above Rydal Water – a dank, eerie hollow so tall that you can stroll into it with the minimum of claustrophobia.

There is a cobweb of paths deviating hither and thither all over the fell, handily serving to disperse its many visitors from Ambleside. Twelve are selected here along with a circular low-level tour for days where there are no views to be had from higher up.

Ascent from Clappersgate 13

From the town, Todd Crag is the first fell-top and certainly a high point in terms of its superb position at the head of Windermere. The most direct route is from Clappersgate.

Via Todd Crag →3.7km/2¼ miles ↑275m/900ft ⊕1hr 30min

1 From the parking spot, walk up to the road junction (left to Langdale, right to Ambleside) and cross with care. A footpath signed from the main road leads up a narrow walled path to a gate then winds up by the 'Sid Cross Memorial Seat', dedicated to the former landlord of the Old Dungeon Ghyll and much-loved doyen of Langdale climbing society who died in 1998 at the age of 85.

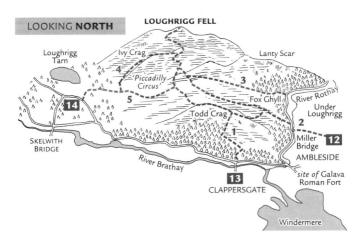

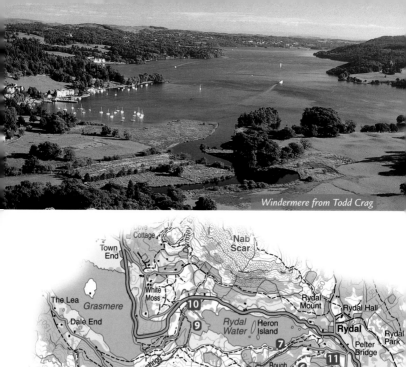

Windermere from Todd Crag

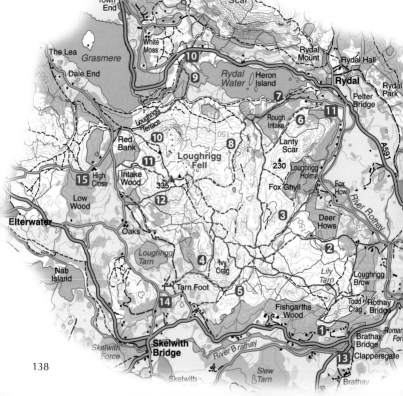

The path leads all the way to **Todd Crag**. The ridge walk from here by **Lily Tarn** is a very pleasing stroll that leads on via a hand-gate in the cross-ridge fence where the enclosure walls bottleneck. Either cross the next knoll or skirt to the left to cross the bridle-path from Pinerigg to Tarn Foot and fall into step with **2**.

Ascent from Ambleside 12

Two straightforward routes set off from central Ambleside over Miller Bridge and lead straight to the heart of the fell. Route 2 can be varied for an extra bit of fell-top interest.

Direct →*3.2km/2 miles* ↑*270m/890ft* ⊕*1hr 15min*
2 Turn left as you leave the Rydal Road car park, following the footway, and then turn left into Stoney Lane (cul-de-sac), which leads onto a path direct to Miller Bridge. Cross **Miller Bridge** and turn right, then take the metalled lane rising left signed to 'Browhead and Pinerigg'. For the most direct route, follow the road and subsequent track via gates above Pinerigg and through the old golf course. When you reach a '**Piccadilly Circus**' of intersecting pathways at the heart of the fell, turn right to climb up from the damp bracken-beset hollow, appropriately known as Black Mire, onto the ridge. Keep straight ahead up a lateral trough to reach the busy summit. Alternatively, take the footpath signed 'Clappersgate' at the first bend above Browhead up the wall steps. Follow this, and pass through a wood to a squeeze-stile, then ascend, keeping left to pass a large cairn – a viewpoint for Ambleside. Advance to a ladder-stile and then onto the prominent top. The second top is the main **Todd Crag** viewpoint. Turn right to continue on with Route **1** to '**Piccadilly Circus**'.

Via Fox Ghyll
→*3.8km/2½ miles* ↑*445m/1460ft* ⊕*1hr 20min*
3 Another straightforward ascent from **Miller Bridge** turns right after the bridge onto the **Under Loughrigg** road but stays on that road for about a kilometre before reaching **Fox Ghyll**. There a footpath is signposted southwest, behind the

house, and runs up beside the gill itself to reach the big 'Piccadilly Circus' path intersection and there turn right to join Route **1**.

Ascent from Tarn Foot 14

A popular route onto the fell begins from the vicinity of the Tarn Foot camp site, close to Loughrigg Tarn.

Via Ivy Crag →*2.2km/1½ miles* ↑*235m/770ft* ⏱*1hr 10min*

4 Follow the bridle-lane leading east from **Tarn Foot** Cottage via two gates. After the second gate with slate sign 'Ambleside' go just 100m, and, with a walled-up gate visible on the right, branch up left through the bracken. Soon you are climbing steeply, with a wall to the left and the **Ivy Crag** ridge above on the right, up the ridge path. Turn left to join **2**.

  5 Or, more simply, keep along the track to the 'Piccadilly Circus' of paths and streams. Bear left onto the ridge, as with **2**.

Ascent from Pelter Bridge 11

The more complete and intimate approaches to Loughrigg begin from Rydal. The back road going west from the car park leads by Steps End into a bridle-lane, the quarry extraction track for Loughrigg Cavern, and paths lead on beyond the cavern to Loughrigg Terrace or down by the shore of Rydal Water.

Via Fox Ghyll, Lanty Scar or Loughrigg Cavern →*3.2km/2 miles* ↑*275m/900ft* ⏱*1hr*

6 Take the footpath signposted left after the entrance to Cote How and before the pair of cottages. Ascend the bank to a gate, now with a wall on the right and handsome views to Nab Scar and the Rydal Beck valley. In high summer the bracken is commensurately high too, but a path exists that runs on by a hand-gate and, when the wall ends, traverses the damp

Cairn on Lanty Scar

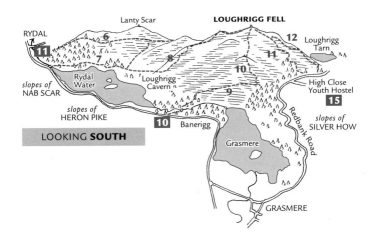

slope to join a path now heading south. A spur path on the left gains the cairn on top of **Lanty Scar**. Continue south over a saddle to reach the 'Piccadilly Circus' path interchange, and go right, climbing above Black Mire onto the ridge proper (**2**) bound for the summit.

7 Take the lane beyond Steps End and, short of the cavern, ascend the valley to link up with Route **6** where it traverses from the wall end, before the **Lanty Scar** spur.

8 Follow Route **7** until you reach **Loughrigg Cavern**. Admire the gaping mouth and try venturing in atop the stepping-stones inside at your own risk! Now head up the bank from the left-hand (east) side of the cave entrance. A path winds up the edge of the ridge to become less than certain as damp hollows are encountered. Either keep south to eventually join up with the main path from Black Mire, or be intrepid and find your own way westward, through the confusion of irregular and fragmented paths that will take you to the top.

Ascent from White Moss 10

Lovely paths lead to Loughrigg Terrace, Loughrigg Cavern and the gentle wood-fringed delights of both Rydal Water and Grasmere.

Via Loughrigg Terrace → 2km/1¼ miles ↑275m/900ft ⏱50min

9 From the car park follow the compacted path to the footbridge. Paths on either side lead upstream to Grasmere lake shore and ultimately to **Redbank Road**. Cross the bridge and head up into the wood ahead, reaching a hand-gate. Go right and embark upon Loughrigg's most treasured possession, the **Terrace** – not a row of industrial housing, but a wonderful path traversing the fellside. Seats en route allow for a prolonged admiration of a stunning composition, with Grasmere seen as a great lake in a bowl of fine fells.

10 Short of the gate into woodland, join the staircase path on the left. Much effort has been employed to give durability to this popular climb. Mount to a ragged cairn, often called the 'Grasmere cairn' for its the prime viewpoint qualities, and continue to the summit knoll set back from the brink. This route can be reached from **Redbank Road**. Unavoidably, approaches from the village of Grasmere are obliged to follow this narrow, windy road, and cars become the hazard for walkers in summer months. A permissive

Loughrigg Fell from Nab Scar

path dips off the road to the left from a hand-gate and steps just beyond Lea Cottage. This leads down to the lake shore then wends delightfully through to open woodland. You can switch back right, up to the lodge, and there switch again to the left in front of the lodge on the cobbled track (avoiding the road altogether). Still within the wood, rise to a gate into a lane, go the few paces left to the gate, and from directly onto **Loughrigg Terrace** and the flight of steps to the top.

Ascent from High Close 15

Redbank Road offers access to Grasmere lake shore, woods and two futher direct lines of ascent, less travelled but equally efficacious.

Via the west ridge or Intake Wood →0.8km/½ mile ↑175m/575ft ⏲30min
11 Leave the car park along the road (northeast) and turn sharply right back southeast from the road fork heading down to **Loughrigg Tarn**. After a few hundred metres, a path leaves the road (no sign) and winds up an open section of slope to a hand-gate. Continue up, eventually with the wall to the right, then go onto the open fell-side, climbing to join the main northwesterly path to the top.

   12 Further south down the minor road, a footpath is signed at a stile beside a cottage. This contours through coniferous woodland via stiles to a cairn short of a gate. Bear immediately left climbing with a gill, and continue direct to the top.

Circular Tour from Pelter Bridge 11

→8km/5 miles ⏲2hr

As a special treat, walkers may forget the summit altogether and entertain a circular tour, a useful option when the fell-top is enveloped in cloud.

Walk south along the **Under Loughrigg** road and branch off right, following the path via hand-gates and entering **Fox Ghyll** (**3**). At the path intersection at the heart of the fell, join the bridle-path from Ambleside crossing under **Ivy Crag** (**4**), with Great Langdale displayed ahead. Descend to **Tarn Foot** Cottage and go right, through the gate, onto the fenced drive above **Loughrigg Tarn**.

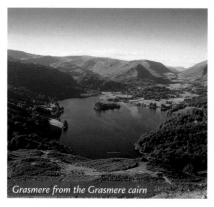
Grasmere from the Grasmere cairn

Either follow the path off right just past the tarn or continue directly to the road. Rise to **Redbank Road** top junction, taking the path in an avenue, signed right, leading down to **Loughrigg Terrace** (**9**). Keep right to visit either **Loughrigg Cavern**, or the **Rydal Water** shore (ultimately joining Route **7**) en route to Pelter Bridge. This is a grand tour with remarkably little ascent.

The summit

A fine stone-built Ordnance Survey column takes pride of place on a rock plinth. Two other contesting tops to the northeast and south fail to claim summit status by a matter of a few feet. The view makes this a place of special attraction, and the panorama in this guide will help you identify the surrounding fells.

Safe descents

There is craggy ground due south from the summit and much muddled cropping out elsewhere. The advice is to stick to the worn paths. They are reliable. The nearest road is due W (**11** or **12**). For Grasmere, White Moss and Rydal follow the NW path (**10**) down to the west end of Loughrigg Terrace. For Ambleside the journey is that much longer. Head SE along the ridge (**2**). The path dips beyond Ivy Crag to join the bridleway E, via Pinerigg (**1**).

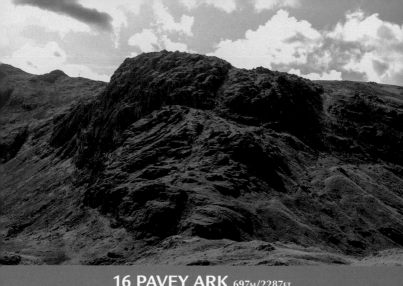

16 PAVEY ARK 697M/2287FT

Climb it from	Stickle Ghyll **17**
Character	Rock writ large – a craggy facade promising rough ascents
Summit grid ref	NY 285 079
Link it with	Harrison Stickle or Thunacar Knott

From the New Dungeon Ghyll Hotel the dark, brooding brow of Pavey Ark can just be seen peering over the corrie lip at the top of Stickle Ghyll. In summer endless processions of people wend up the much-strengthened path to behold, awestruck, the mighty walls across the steely waters of Stickle Tarn. For many the view is sufficient. Others, with measured confidence, orbit the tarn and ascend the scree to tackle the rock-ladder of Jack's Rake (**8**).

On this route hands and feet are in action all the way, on the firmest of rock, with remarkably few moments of real exposure to daunt the spirit. It is a uniquely wonderful opportunity for the average fellwalker to experience the thrill of a classic Lakeland cliff. But beware – it does become increasingly serious in wind and rain, and in winter conditions reverts to the sole preserve of roped mountaineers.

↑ The eastern aspect of Pavey Ark

For those who would rather not use their hands, the North Rake (7) provides the one direct ascent for the fellwalker, climbing from Bright Beck to the east. Pavey Ark can also be reached via Harrison Combe (6) and there are a clutch of options to choose from for getting to the glorious Stickle Tarn on the way.

Ascent from Stickle Ghyll 17

Via Pike How →2.5km/1½ miles ↑610m/2000ft ⏱1hr 10min

An excellent ascent, away from the busyness of Stickle Ghyll, with fine views

Either go directly up the bridle-path from the hotel or ascend from Stickle Ghyll car park information shelter. The paths meet up by the fence-gap.

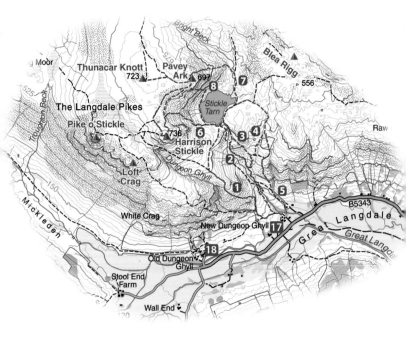

1 The Pike How route leads off left from the fence-gap and rises to a hand-gate where you turn right, passing a seat to a stile. Keep the wall to the right, and do not ford **Dungeon Ghyll**. The well-marked path bears left, mounting the steep slope in steady stages. Much of the path has been re-engineered to cope with the inevitable heavy foot traffic. Many walkers use this as their return leg after the ascent via Stickle Ghyll, though they would be better resorting to the Mark Gate path off **Loft Crag**, as it has the best base. Climbing up to the saddle behind **Pike How**, make a move to the right to stand on top. It is a splendid viewpoint for Great Langdale. While the main path angles west-northwest a useful lesser path leads along the rim of the slope on a right-hand curve to reach the **Stickle Tarn** dam. This route gives a fine view across the gulf of Stickle Ghyll to Tarn Crag.

Tortuous pitched trail climbing Stickle Ghyll

Via Stickle Ghyll to Stickle Tarn →*1.6km/1 mile* ↑*430m/1410ft* ⏱*1hr*

Four different routes to this iconic Langdale tarn, in descending order of popularity.

2 Go straight up the paved rock path beside the tree-shaded section of Stickle Ghyll. Cross the footbridge and rise to a stile. Keep to the right-hand side of the valley – the paths to the west are in a poor state, so give them a miss. Stepping through a fold, wind up the rigg between small fenced conifer saplings to reach a fine four-part waterfall. At this point there are two options. The first is to continue up the gill, negotiating a rock-step and rising to a ford, and then complete the climb directly at **Stickle Tarn** dam. Alternatively, **3** ascend the well-made stone stair which zig-zags to a higher level before angling left onto a shelf beneath **Tarn Crag** to rejoin Route **2**.

    4 Or, to extend your ascent by a quieter route, follow the turf trail continuation past the left-swinging turnoff (**3**) further up the fell. Keep to the right of the **Tarn Crag** outcrops, with a roofless shelter on the left and an isolated walled enclosure to the right. Cross over the shoulder to reach **Stickle Tarn** at its eastern end.

5 A far more pleasant line begins directly after leaving the New Dungeon Ghyll. Cross the footbridge located half-right after the initial gate. The path runs up behind Millbeck Farm and enters a lane via a hand-gate, and then rises from the wall onto the bracken ridge. Avoid outcrops by slanting left. Either contour onto the main zig-zagging path or climb, with tenuous initial evidence of a path in the bracken. On finding the green path skirt the right-hand shoulder of a knoll above a steep gill. Subsequently traverse the walled enclosure diagonally to a narrow wall-gap and join up with the upper section of the old shepherds' path. This passes walled boulders and slips over a saddle depression to meet the path running along the eastern shore of the tarn from the outflow. Ahead, the massive eastern face of Pavey Ark smiles down upon the cool, dark waters of the tarn.

From Stickle Tarn to the summit → *1.3km/¾ mile* ↑*235m/770ft* ⏱ *1hr 15min*

There are three popular lines of ascent for the fellwalker from the dam – left towards Harrison Combe (Route 6), right via the North Rake (Route 7) and – for those happy with hands-on walking – straight on round the tarn to the infamous Jack's Rake (Route 8).

6 Go left on the obvious path. Work up the loose slope to the right of the buttresses of **Harrison Stickle**. Go right on meeting the higher contouring path, venture onto the distinctively coarse-rock ridge and clamber through the crag-shielding wall onto the summit.

Stickle Tarn and Pavey Ark

149

Looking up to the ash tree on the notorious Jack's Rake

7 Go right from the dam along the shore path to follow, then ford, Bright Beck and mount the prominent gully or rake up the east ridge. This is North Rake. All too often used as a line of descent, it has inevitably become badly eroded. Gaining the ridge-top, the path swings round by the broken wall and passes a pooled hollow to gain the summit from the northwest.

8 Jack's Rake, along with the tiny climb onto Helm Crag's summit outcrop, marks the zenith of fellwalking technical difficulty and endeavour in the central Lake District. Paths approach from either side of the tarn. That by the west shore is the old-time favourite, climbing the scree slope from the northwest edge of the tarn via a prominent memorial cairn inscribed 'S.W.S. 1900'. The eastern approach (not marked on map) crosses possibly the looser scree, but by keeping up to the right, early on, and by a deft slight of foot, you can avoid almost all of the scree! The two approaches converge at the very centre of the cliff base.

There are five distinct stages to the climb. It would be an over-elaboration to call them 'pitches', as the groove offers several opportunities to take a breath at an ash tree and a patch of thistles. It features a squeeze behind a fallen splinter of rock, the Gun, and concludes above Great Gully, dipping momentarily, then scrambling up rock slabs to the wall end above a projecting rock. The instinct to climb being well developed by now you will naturally find a scrambly way to the top, brushing aside all notion of linking to the ridge path.

Do not be seduced by 'Easy Gully', which angles up to the right from the scree slope, unless you are confident on rock. Jack's Rake is accessible to anyone who can climb a stepladder but this route is not.)

The summit

All trace of a cairn has been lost, and the bare rock top has little need of one. The rocks themselves are fascinating igneous exposures, displaying intricately confused patterns. There is one large perched erratic boulder just to the south, and a few pools on the north and west sides enhance the rock-garden effect. The view is not the best in Langdale but the imminence of an immense cliff under your feet conveys a sense of tingling drama.

Safe descents

North Rake (**7**), despite being loose in parts, is a secure line of retreat. Head slightly NNW from the top, passing through the wall, and the well-defined path curves to the right into the rake, bound for Stickle Tarn's east shore. Don't 'bound', however, as a steady stride will be kinder on the trail!

Ridge routes

Harrison Stickle →*0.8km/½ mile* ↓*10m/33ft* ↑*60m/200ft* ⏱*25min*
This peak is in view from the outset. The consistent path runs just under the edge, avoids the ridge-top rock tors, links with the path climbing from the south shore of Stickle Tarn, and rises, with two paths mounting either from the east or north. There is scope for good sport in following the ridge-top all the way. Although the path is intermittent, the final grassy rise to the summit is quite trouble free.

Thunacar Knott →*0.5km/¼ mile* ↓*10m/33ft* ↑*30m/100ft* ⏱*15min*
A clear path leads off W, curving NW and aiming for the depression at the head of Bright Beck. Take an early deviation to the left, with no trace of a path, and attain the summit cairn short of the pool.

17 PIKE O'BLISCO 705m/2313ft

Climb it from	Old Dungeon Ghyll **18**, Blea Tarn **20**, Castle Howe **21** or Wrynose Pass **22**
Character	Great individualist with a tiered rock-cake summit
Fell-friendly route	7
Summit grid ref	NY 271 042
Link it with	Cold Pike
Part of	The Great Langdale Round

There is energy in the name Pike o'Blisco, neatly matching the fell's sharply chiselled profile, particularly when viewed from Great Langdale. Defined by Oxendale to the north and Blea Tarn beneath the formidable facade of Blake Rigg to the east, the rough southeastern slopes are known as Wrynose Fell, sitting as they do above Wrynose Beck, and the southern slopes run down to the Wrynose Pass road. The moraine hollow of Red Tarn and Browney Gill ravine make up the western boundary.

Overlooking Oxendale two bold crags – Kettle Crag and Black Wars – deny access to the fellwalker but strong walkers will see the fell as the first, or last, port of call on a grand circuit of the head of Great Langdale. Offering a splendid

↑ *Pike o'Blisco from Crinkle Crags*

view, not least of Crinkle Crags, in its own right, the summit is also a historic landmark. Up until 1974, the old Cumberland county boundary made a darting visit to the southern cairn, taking a 35 degree slice out of Westmorland before falling back over Black Crag to Wrynose Pass, where the two counties came face to face with Lancashire. And the only example of a Viking 'moot' in Lakeland, the Ting Mound, sits at the southeast corner of the fell (visit https://historicengland. co.uk for more information) at Castle Howe.

This is another fine fell with something for everyone from almost all directions: Routes 1–3 from the north, Route 4–6 from the east and Route 7–9 from the south.

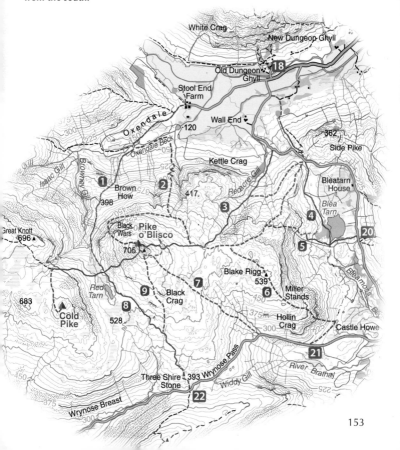

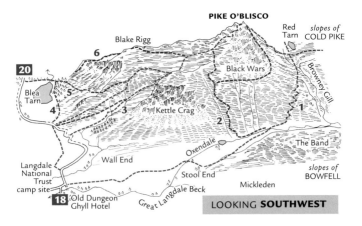

LOOKING SOUTHWEST

Ascent from Old Dungeon Ghyll 18

*A choice of three contrasting northern approaches – two graded and easy to
follow and one for the wandering spirit, steeply up on intermittent sheep trods
with the option of a bit of scrambling at the end (Route 2).*

Via Browney Gill or Skull Gill →4.7km/3 miles ↑610m/2000ft ⏱2hr 20min
1 Follow the farm-road leading to, and through, **Stool End**. Keep to the track
into **Oxendale** leading, via a sheepfold gangway, to the footbridge. After
the bridge, the popular path continues, via the stone-pitched staircase, on a
southwesterly line. Climb over a rigg, keeping above the **Browney Gill** ravine,
to reach the pass short of **Red Tarn**. Turn sharp left to complete the ascent.

2 There is a middle way, seldom considered, leading up the rigg by Skull
Gill. From the footbridge bear left along the damp valley floor. As the delta
debris of Skull Gill draws near, angle up right towards **Kettle Crag**. Reaching
the ravine, bear right on a faint shepherds' trod. The zig-zags dissolve far too
soon as the smooth rigg rears. At the top, either continue through the cor-
rugated terrain to meet up with the main ridge path, or, drift right, holding to
sheep trods drawing tightly under **Black Wars**. Slip under the tilted buttress,
hugging the base of outcropping rising up a shelf. There are options to clamber onto the rocks, but the shelf serves well. Either continue to link up with

the path ascending from **Red Tarn** or angle left to climb the final arete direct to the summit.

Via Redacre Gill →4.7km/3 miles ↑520m/1700ft ⊕2hr

3 The conventional approach leads south from the Old Dungeon Ghyll, follows the road beyond **Wall End**, squeezes by a roadside barn, crosses a cattle grid and then winds up the hill. At the third bend a clear path leads off right. This is the main route up the **Redacre Gill** valley.

The path is well-marked and after fording three gills becomes beautifully pitched rising steeply onto the plateau. (As a variation follow the footpath leading up from the camp site to the ladder-stile onto the road pass. Go straight over the road, sweeping round the rigg ahead on a southwesterly course contouring to join the Redacre path.) The path ascends to the right of a large block slab. Weave up, via a tangle of routes through rock bands, to gain the summit.

Ascent from Blea Tarn 20

Blea Tarn is in many respects the better place to start with a choice of three lines up the fell.

From the north east →4km/2½ miles ↑660m/2165ft ⊕1hr 30min

4 The path leading north from the Blea Tarn plantation arrives at a ladder-stile at the road pass. Here you can choose the contouring path to Redacre Gill (**3**) or turn south to ascend the ridge, keeping a right-hand bias.

Direct →3km/2 miles ↑550m/1805ft ⊕1hr 10min

5 The same ridge can be reached more energetically direct from the plantation, on a clear grass path climbing to cross a stile in the skyline fence. Traverse the slope and on meeting the minor ridge path, angle up across a

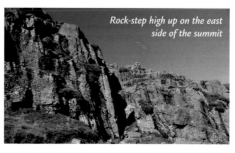
Rock-step high up on the east side of the summit

scarred bank to emerge on the edge, then contour to join the Redacre path (**3**) where it reaches the moor.

Ascent from Castle Howe 21

From Little Langdale the Wrynose road winds up by Fell Foot. Directly after Castle Howe the traveller's attention is struck by the beautiful view of the Langdale Pikes through the Blea Tarn gap. This is another ascent for the explorer and great fun!

Via Blake Rigg →*3.2km/2 miles* ↑*515m/1690ft* ⏲*1hr 30min*
6 At the wall corner of the parking area a footpath is signed right. Follow this path around the marsh/bracken fringe. Step off the path to climb the pathless, blunt ridge. A finger of bracken extends up this southeast ridge of **Blake Rigg**, giving a clue to the key ramp higher up that gives easy access to the top of **Miller Stands**. The continuing ridge mounts onto Blake Rigg, giving scope to enjoy excellent views over Blea Tarn to Lingmoor Fell. A prominent cairn marks the top. There is no path across the marshy ridge, interrupted by occasional outcroppings, to meet Route **4**.

Via Wrynose Beck →*2.7km/1¾ miles* ↑*510m/1670ft* ⏲*1hr 25min*
7 Walk up the **Wrynose Pass** road to cross Wrynose Bridge, bear off right on an evident path which accompanies Wrynose Beck to its marshy source and beyond mounts the craggy final feet to the fell summit.

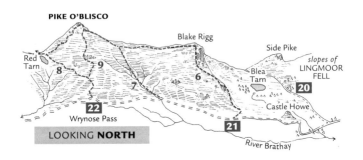

Crinkle Crags and Bowfell from the summit

Ascent from Wrynose Pass 22

With the ascent reduced to a tad over a thousand feet, many walkers choose this approach.

Via Red Tarn →2.4km/1½ miles ↑315m/1030ft ⏱1hr

8 The path is never in doubt, being a popular approach for Crinkle Crags via the marshy hollow wherein **Red Tarn** resides. Soon after the tarn, bear up right (**1**) at an obvious cross-paths.

Via Black Crag →2km/1¼ miles ↑315m/1030ft ⏱50min

9 The more attractive option veers right, on the early rise by a fenced fold attached to a large erratic boulder. The path winds up the bank to pass **Black Crag** (notice the needle rock). The cairn on the top is worth visiting and the cairn on the southern summit pike is easily gained through the final outcrops.

The summit

The ultimate ground is reminiscent of a battleship with cannon-station cairns at the north prow and southern aft, set on an irregular bare rock deck. The northern cairn, the summit, has had a hard life, and deserves to be reconstructed more durably. Visitors to the summit perch on many a ledge to witness a particularly fine view, Crinkle Crags receiving most admiration.

Safe descents

The easiest escape is SW. A popular path (**1**) descends to the depression N of Red Tarn. Either follow the path N (**1**), by rough steps initially beside the headstream of Browney Gill, then over a rigg shoulder onto a pitched stair-case leading down to the footbridge in Oxendale, bound for Stool End, or go SE (**8**), passing Red Tarn to reach the road at the top of Wrynose Pass. E from the summit, a tortuous mangle of paths seeks various lines of weakness via a series of rock bands, none of which is too terrible. They all coalesce on the regular path to Redacre Gill (**3**). Descend easily until the steep gill is entered, fortunately now well furnished with stone stair pitching.

Ridge route

Cold Pike →2km/1¼ miles ↓200m/670ft ↑200m/670ft ⊕35min
Follow the popular path SW down to the depression. Ford the gill, continuing W on an easy gradient, crossing a small patch of exposed red soil. As the path shapes to ford a gill issuing from the moor, bear off left, ascending directly to the summit – a matching twin with Pike o'Blisco.

The Coniston Fells from the summit

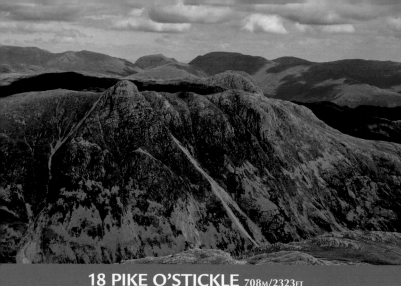

18 PIKE O'STICKLE 708m/2323ft

Climb it from	Old Dungeon Ghyll **18**
Character	Perhaps the most iconic rocky-knob summit of all
Summit grid ref	NY 274 074
Link it with	Loft Crag or Thunacar Knott
Part of	The Langdale Pikes

Pike o'Stickle both provides the backdrop to the familiar view of the Langdale Pikes from Great Langdale and cheekily pokes up to tease on an otherwise quite feature-free skyline in views from the north, on the Borrowdale flank of the range. It is made of a particularly hard igneous rock, which was highly valuable to Neolithic tool-makers some 4000–6000 years ago, who quarried the South Scree to make top-notch axes, traded throughout the British Isles. The valley track they followed is now believed to have featured a shrine, on the large erratics below Copt How, where stylised blessings (rock-art), only identified as recently as 1999, were pecked out with axes.

South Scree is no longer a place to venture but there are many other ways to visit and admire Pike o'Stickle close up, eschewing the ever-popular Stickle Tarn. The two lonelier routes outlined here approach from magnificent Mickleden.

↑ *Pike o'Stickle from Bowfell*   159

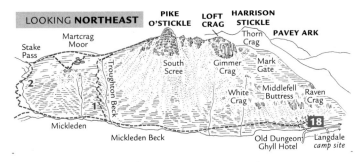

Ascent from Old Dungeon Ghyll 18

As the object of a climb Pike o'Stickle is often reached at the tail-end of a tour of the Pikes but it can worthily be ascended directly by these two northwestern approaches.

Via Mickleden →5.2km/3¼ miles ↑655m/2150ft ⊕2hr 45min
1 Pass up behind the hotel to the kissing-gate and follow the valley track, via a further kissing-gate, where the broad lane opens into Mickleden. Stride along the floor of this grand mountain arena with Gimmer Crag and Pike o'Stickle eye-catching features up to the right, while Pike o'Blisco, the Band, Bowfell and Rossett Pike rise to the left and ahead. The well-graded track helps mountain rescue vehicles to approach the foot of Rossett Gill. Pass under Pike o'Stickle, glancing up at the ribbon of unstable scree spilling from the south gully. Neither ascent nor descent by this line should be considered. It is in a dire state.

Seek **Troughton Beck**, the tumbling, stony watercourse (frequently dry in summer) issuing from the open ravine high up the fell, spanned by stone flags. Ascend on the west side, skirting the flood boulders, and a well-used and well-maintained path soon comes into view. Wind up the bracken slope. Climbing well above the gill it provides suitably handsome views. Once the moor brink is attained, follow the beck on a less distinct path, until a natural fording point lets you sweep half-left to a cairn to join the popular path from **Stake Pass**. Go right, and the path duly curving right avails itself of the boulders to cross a particularly peaty patch, then climbs easily to the brow to be confronted by the final rocky stage of Pike o'Stickle. You'll need to use your hands to reach the top! There are several scrambly paths to choose from.

Via Stake Pass →7km/4¼ miles ↑670m/2200ft ⊕3hr
2 A few paces on from **Troughton Beck** (**1**) notice the poignant plaque to Jim Dearden, installed by his 'best mate', and feel an immediate empathy for a fellow fellwalker. Continue to the simple footbridge crossing **Stake Gill**, and a stone indicates left to Rossett Gill and right for Stake Pass. Bear right, and from the sheepfold the old pass winds up the slope away from the beck, then comes closer to it again higher up, from where Pike o'Stickle looks strikingly solitary. The view down Mickleden is memorable, while across the dale head admire the high buttresses of Bowfell. Fording the beck the path winds along the moraine on the eastern side of **Langdale Combe**, the site of a former tarn.

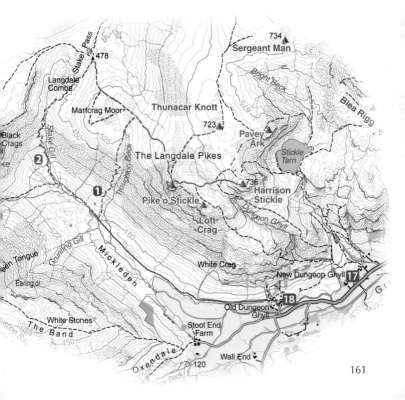

Some 50m short of the cairn marking the top of **Stake Pass**, reach a junction with a path leading left, bound for **Rossett Pike**.

Go right, mounting the often wet slope on a strong path that skirts several marshes en route to the cairn on the main slope, encountered on Route 1. An attractive loop can be created by wandering south to the rocky summit of **Martcrag Moor** – no finer place exists to study the craggy face of Bowfell. A crude shelter has been built by walkers in need of a wild-country bivouac among the large boulders, while several pools adorn the plateau, giving scope for camera action towards Pike o'Stickle. Just past Martcrag Moor, Route **1** joins from the right. Follow it on to the summit.

The summit

Pike o'Stickle from Loft Crag

A cairn rests atop the airy location, with plenty of space for a small party to sit at ease. This is one of the treasured places in the Central Fells, living up to the great expectations. The gulf of Mickleden gives scale to Bowfell and Pike o'Blisco. But the most exciting subject is near neighbour Loft Crag, buttressed by Gimmer Crag.

Safe descents

Your first move must be N to the foot of the stack, and you will have judged, during your scrambling ascent, that this cannot be undertaken speedily. For Langdale follow the prominent path E down into Harrison Combe. Here, once across the ghyll, look for the good path on the right which can be followed clearly all the way down to skirt right round Pike How and continue down to the valley bottom.

From above Langdale Combe

Ridge routes

Loft Crag →*0.4km/¼ mile* ↓*60m/200ft* ↑*25m/80ft* ⏱*15min*
Descend N off the stack, then follow the obvious ridge to the SE, not the clear
path which drifts down into Harrison Combe, to reach the summit.

Thunacar Knott →*0.8km/½ mile* ↓*55m/180ft* ↑*70m/230ft* ⏱*25min*
From the foot of the stack head N (no path), off the line of the path to Stake
Pass. Traverse the spongy depression to link up with the narrow path, running
up the slope W–E, bound for the summit.

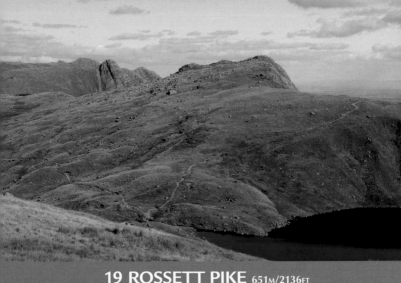

19 ROSSETT PIKE 651M/2136FT

Climb it from	Old Dungeon Ghyll **18** or Stonethwaite **2**
Character	An easy-to-climb shoulder ridge connection between ranges
Fell-friendly route	1 or 2
Summit grid ref	NY 249 076
Link it with	Pike o'Stickle
Part of	The Great Langdale Round

In the company of so magnificent an array of peaks, Rossett Pike may be thought a minor player but it forms a conclusive headwall to the classic 'U'-shaped glacial valley of Mickleden. The moraine directly beneath is characteristic of this glacial origin, as is the amazing collection of pillow moraines in the hanging valley of Langdale Combe.

The easily gained summit can give a truncated day some sense of achievement when higher brethren are wreathed in mist and worse, accessed by either of the contrasting age-old pony paths. Being at such a vantage point on this great valley-head, it is also an excellent place from which to survey either Bowfell or the Langdale Pikes on days when the weather is kinder.

⬆ *From above Angle Tarn*

In addition to the two well-worn routes up from Mickleden (1–3), two more routes lead up from Borrowdale via Langstrath (4–5), should you be wanting to take a more unconventional approach.

Ascent from Old Dungeon Ghyll **18** *off map E*

It is unusual to be able to start a fell walk in the central Lake District with almost an hour of flowing strides and there is plenty to admire on the long, flat walk-in to these routes.

Via Mickleden and Rossett Gill →*5km/3 miles* ↑*555m/1820ft* ⏱*1hr 50min*

1 Mickleden has negligible gradient but it's impossible not to be awestruck as you proceed along the bridleway from behind the hotel craning your neck up at Gimmer Crag and Pike o'Stickle. Bowfell grudgingly reveals its prized craggy possessions high to your left, Bowfell Buttress a distant object of admiration. Rossett Pike, on the other hand, contrives to dominate the dale head itself, a simple focus of attention. If the cloud is sufficiently low to obscure the crags of Bowfell, then Rossett Pike will seem alone, now all the more likely a fell-walk scalp. Where you cross the footbridge at the bottom of **Stake Gill** a slate sign marks the fork in the bridleway.

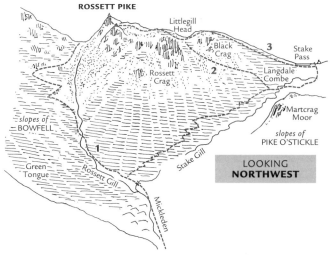

ROSSETT PIKE

Littlegill Head

Black Crag

3

Stake Pass

Rossett Crag

2

Langdale Combe

Martcrag Moor

slopes of BOWFELL

slopes of PIKE O'STICKLE

1

Green Tongue

Rossett Gill

Stake Gill

LOOKING **NORTHWEST**

Mickleden

A left turn traverses up to a fording point in **Rossett Gill** from where a smart pitched path leads up a double zig-zag to the head of Rossett Gill. Forget all thoughts of ascending the gill itself. Many are the walkers who, in the past, have scrabbled up leaving a sad, ugly, unstable mess. Advance to the level ground of the saddle and bear up right onto the easy ridge – it couldn't be sweeter!

Via Stake Pass →6km/3¾ miles ↑555m/1820ft ⏱2hr 10min

2 At the footbridge at the bottom of **Stake Gill**, turn right as signed for 'Stake Pass' and then the turning starts in earnest. The path, engineered in the tightest hair-pins imaginable, winds up under **Black Crag**. As the path shapes to ford the beck, on entry to the hanging valley of **Langdale Combe**, branch immediately left. Take the path climbing directly up the grassy slope. This mounts onto a grassy shelf and, with the encouragement of small cairns, traverses above Black Crag to **Littlegill Head**. A path climbs from this saddle, keeping to the ridge-top which is comfortably rough, to reach the summit.

Upper section of pitched path by Rossett Gill

3 Ford **Stake Gill** with the main path and continue with the old bridleway as it curves round the wide hollow of **Langdale Combe**, littered with an amazing collection of glacial moraine hummocks. A cairn marks the top of **Stake Pass** (1575ft/478m). Turn left (west), skirting a large peaty pool, which is only redeemed when sunlight, sky and cloud are reflected in its otherwise unscenic waters. There is a strong path curving round the head of the combe. You may notice a 'retired path' forking right to contour the upper slope, but don't use it. It needs to heal and the ridge path to the top is far more scenic anyway.

Ascent from Stonethwaite **2** *off map N*

Via Langstrath →*8.7km/5¼ miles* ↑*560m/1840ft* ⏱*3hr*

For many walkers, including those on the Cumbria Way, Langstrath is a means not an end, a delightfully scenic through-route link from Borrowdale to Great Langdale. But you can use it for a ridge-top (Route 4) or valley (Route 5) ascent of Rossett Pike, too.

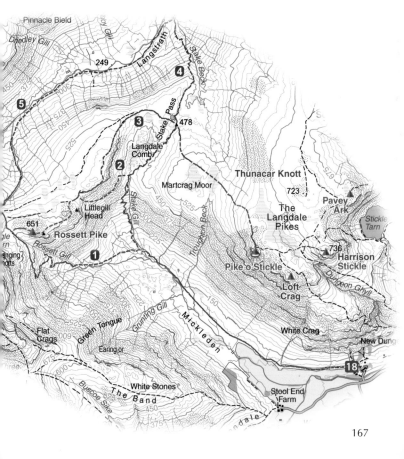

4 The Cumbria Way chooses the bridleway on the east side of the valley. The better path is the footpath on the west side which crosses Tray Dub and **Stake Beck** footbridges. The ascent is enlivened hugely by the vibrant cascades of Stake Beck, then becomes engrossed in the technical twists of the upper section of the path. You don't have to wait for the pass-top cairn to branch onto the ridge but it will guide you to the most consistent path. The natural ridge path (Route **3**), mounting onto the crest above **Black Crag**, dips into **Littlegill Head** and then becomes rougher on Buck Pike above **Rossett Crag** leading to the east cairn.

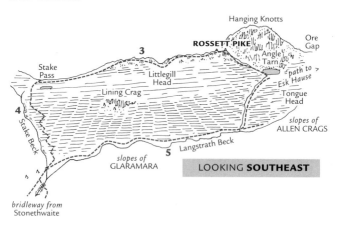

5 When you cross **Stake Beck** footbridge you can keep in the valley tracking up the narrowing dale with at least one fine waterfall in view below. At the confluence with Angletarn Gill, find a convenient ford. Even in summer a sudden downpour can make it impossible to cross here in which case the south bank has to suffice. The popular path ascends to the outflow of **Angle Tarn**, turns left on the regular path to the saddle, then veers half-left onto the summit.

The summit

A rocky east/west crest, this is the perfect place from which to survey the cliffs of Bowfell, with the great slab of Flat Crags prominent, and the east cairn is a

Swift path from Angle Tarn to Stake Pass

lofty perch from which to comprehend the relationship of the Langdale Pikes with Mickleden.

Safe descents

Backtrack W to the saddle and follow the Rossett Gill bridleway (**1**) left.

Ridge route

Pike o'Stickle →4.2km/2½ miles ↓180m/590ft ↑240m/790ft ⏱1hr 20min
Wedded to the Mid-Western group, yet for most walkers intrinsic to the Great Langdale circuit, this is the natural and popular ridge connection. Follow the ridge NE to Stake Pass. A clear path continues from the cairn on a line S over the marshy Martcrag Moor. From the head of Troughton Beck a cairned path has been consolidated to the northern base of the famous pike. The summit is gained only by hands-on scrambling.

20 SCAFELL PIKE 977M/3206FT

Climb it from	Old Dungeon Ghyll **18**, Seathwaite **1**, Wasdale Head Village Green **28**, Brotherilkeld **25** or Wha House **26**
Character	Remote and rugged, daunting and deserving of great respect
Fell-friendly Route	4
Summit grid ref	NY 215 072
Link it with	Great End, Scafell or Lingmell
Part of	The Roof of England

Scafell Pike must be the monarch of all Lakeland mountains, following hard on the heels of Helvellyn as the most popular climb of the major fells. It is, in every dimension, a real mountain. Crag and scree abound on all fronts meaning that care is needed both in ascent and descent and the summit contrives to keep itself remote from the gaze of valley observers.

It is not the most beautiful, does not have the very best ascent, does not offer the finest panorama and is not home to the most challenging crags, but Scafell Pike is the highest, roughest, toughest and assuredly the most revered ground. In a district simply bristling with shapely peaks there is inevitably a strong impulse to stand atop the highest of the lot.

↑ *Scafell Pike from Bowfell*

Your judgement on when to go, and by which route, needs to be tempered with much forethought. The fell can be climbed from four directions: Wasdale Head (5–7), Seathwaite in Borrowdale (2–4), Great Langdale via Esk Hause (1) and lonely Eskdale (8–10). There are two hot-favourite ascents. Two paths come together in the vicinity of Lingmell Col, from Lingmell Gill (6) and the Corridor Route (2). The other popular approach is from Great Langdale via Rossett Gill and Esk Hause (1). Being closer to the M6 this route comes under disproportionate pressure, but it is nonetheless a grand route.

Ascent from the Old Dungeon Ghyll **18** *off map E*

Scafell Pike is a distant, almost surreal, notion from the Old Dungeon Ghyll, with the added fear that it may be lost in the clouds. The adage 'better to travel hopefully' applies, as too 'retreat is the better part of valour', an option if, having reached Esk Hause, it is, indeed, befogged.

Via Rossett Gill and Esk Hause → *11km/6¾ miles* ↑*955m/3130ft* ⏱*5hr*

1 Starting from the Old Dungeon Ghyll, you can soon pick up your stride in Mickleden but don't overdo it – energy levels will be tested today. Crossing the footbridge at the foot of Stake Gill, engage on the pony path which fords Rossett Gill, then via an exaggerated double zig-zag steps ascend to the saddle at the head of the gill. The path goes down to the outflow of **Angle Tarn**, a place to pause and study the reflections of Hanging Knotts in the hanging waters. The continuing path rises northwestward up **Tongue Head**.

Closing in on the saddle, drift half-left to the cross-wall shelter. This is an important landmark and its existence is no coincidence. The terrain here has a nasty habit of confusing even confident ramblers and it is a meeting of the winds too! Be aware there are two saddles – the east–west link to **Sprinkling Tarn** and **Sty Head** and the higher col of **Esk Hause**, situated 250m to the southwest of the wind-shelter. Esk Hause, the broad depression between **Esk Pike** and Great End, is littered with cairns. Clearly many people come this way bound for Calf Cove. Go west on the all-too-palpable trail. The path winds up the damp hollow wherein lies a small shelter and the last running water.

Climb onto the plateau saddle. So far so good, but the terrain is about to deteriorate. The ridge draws up southwestward to an innominate rocky crest. Weave through the boulders, the path inevitably vague. The boulders

Broad Crag summit (photo: Anne Bowskill)

relent as the summit of Scafell Pike comes tantalisingly into eye shot – more distant than you may have hoped! Here the path sweeps majestically over the gravelly shoulder of the **Ill Crag** plateau, dipping into Illcrag Col, before yet more boulders on the traverse of the east shoulder of **Broad Crag** into Broadcrag Col. Views from the col, left down Little Narrowcove to Pen and right to Lingmell, are quite stirring. Wearying legs need to make one final effort on the sorely eroded scramble up the narrow arête leading to the summit boulder-field. All but the keenest walkers will dally on the summit, perhaps wandering to the various plateau brinks for differing perspectives, knowing that long, rough crossing has to be repeated.

Sadly the tiresome trek across the plateau causes most walkers to ignore Ill Crag and Broad Crag, both considered part and parcel of the Scafell Pike ensemble. In fact, they fully deserve the attention of well-informed fellwanderers and the high-country connoisseur. Broad Crag is a serious adjunct, serious in its utter rockiness. You can count the grass by the blade! The cairn-less top lies only a matter of metres to the west of the ridge path, with easiest access from the north. Ill Crag is actually quite a separate entity as you clearly appreciate if you view it from Pen across Little Narrowcove, removed but at one with the mountainous setting.

Ascent from Seathwaite 1 *off map N*

For all its tantalising distance from the target summit a circular expedition can easily be created courtesy of the paths that fork at Stockley Bridge. The valley

174

to the left (4) leads to Esk Hause, while that to the right (2) makes unerringly for Styhead Pass, thereby joining the Corridor Route.

Via Styhead Pass and the Corridor Route →6.7km/4¼ miles ↑855m/2800ft ⏱4hr 15min

2 From Seathwaite Farm follow the regular bridleway via **Stockley Bridge**. This bears up right via gates climbing above the trees of **Taylorgill Force**, with excellent pitching underpinning a heavily used trail. Though the way is stony on the approach to the **Styhead Gill** footbridge, a more comfortable trail ensues passing **Styhead Tarn** to reach the pass, identified by the stretcher box.

There is nothing passage-like about the **Corridor Route**: it is a deceptively long and quite tough traverse, frequently congested with human traffic. Ongoing pitching works on the steep open sections have made it more comfortable. You can start directly from the Sty Head stretcher box, angling half-left, short-cutting across the headstream of **Spouthead Gill**, but it's better to take the original route which branches right after the initial rise on the eastbound path, as to **Sprinkling Tarn**. Cross the vestige of a short wall, dipping and contouring to the mouth of the **Skew Gill** ravine. Climb the facing slope, pass through a short cutting on a hard staircase rising to a ridge crossing. Beware: the far-side step down is awkward. The path weaves on by two headstream fords of **Greta Gill** before a parting in the way.

Bear right to continue on the Corridor Route and ford **Piers Gill** just where it spills almost innocently into its notoriously deep and treacherous ravine. Eschew the dubious trace of a path that branches up the rough northern slopes west of Dropping Crag. The main path avoids the Lingmell Col. Work up among the outcrops to link with the path from **Hollow Stones** on the broad, stony, but otherwise unthreatening, northwest ridge to the summit.

3 Or, at the junction just after **Greta Gill**, take a clear set of steps to the left which marks the start of a less than savoury direct route to Broadcrag col. The latter stages of the climb up the wild combe to the narrow, rough saddle will test your tempo and temper. The route to the summit (**1**) lies up the blunt eroded arête to the right.

Via Esk Hause →6.5km/4 miles ↑905m/2970ft ⏱4hr 40min

4 The Esk Hause route follows the left-hand path from Stockley Bridge up **Grains Gill**, which becomes **Ruddy Gill** after a footbridge. Pitching is evident right up to the point where the upper ravine is forded. Link to the path rising from **Sprinkling Tarn** and **Sty Head**. Take the first path branching right, leading up to Esk Hause to join Route **1**.

Ascent from Wasdale Head 27 or Wasdale Head Village Green 28

Via Styhead Pass and the Corridor Route →5.7km/3½ miles ↑915m/3000ft ⏱4hr 30min

The direct route up from the head of Wasdale, with a choice of a steady ascent or a pleasant valley approach to Styhead Pass.

5 Leave the village green car park, following the lane by St Olaf's to **Burnthwaite**. Pass to the left among the farm buildings to a gate. Keep right – the obvious way heads on between varying walls, via a gate, to cross a footbridge spanning **Gable Beck**. Soon you face a choice of routes. Both are equally sound routes to Sty Head. The standard route sticks religiously to the

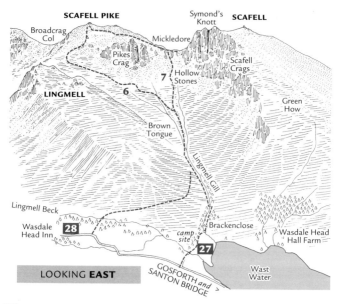

LOOKING **EAST**

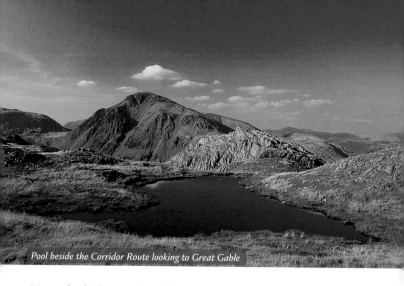

Pool beside the Corridor Route looking to Great Gable

rising path which passes through a hand-gate before taking on the scree section. The passage of several hundred years has ensured a well-defined shelf has been padded down and, but for one brief stumbly section, and a good deal of ball-bearing gravel, the path delivers the walker with minimal fuss.

The more pleasant option lies up the valley. Either bear off as bracken begins to encroach or wait a further hundred metres to find a clear path slanting down to the hand-gate near the foot of the descending wall. Keep alongside **Lingmell Beck**, fording the stream just after the confluence with **Piers Gill**. A clear green trail winds up the rigg, then fords to the left a gill. Cut across the next rigg to ford **Spouthead Gill** and then zig-zag up to **Styhead Pass** to join Route **2**.

Via Lingmell Gill →4.5km/2¾ miles ↑915m/3000ft ◷3hr

Route 6 offers the shortest and most trouble-free ascent, while Route 7 up to Mickledore will involve discomfort, if short-lived, and with no navigational difficulty. The latter path may never have been all that sweet, but certainly the relentless scouring of fell boots has taken its toll.

6 There are two prime approaches to the Lingmell Gill valley. Direct from the NT camp site, follow the path left off the **Wasdale Head Hall** track by

Brackenclose, rising beside the beck to a footbridge and subsequent hand-gates. From the village green follow the road back to the first bend where a stile and footpath sign direct across the dale floor to a footbridge spanning the stony-bedded **Lingmell Beck**. The path bears right, gradually ascending across the fellside to draw over the ridge-end contouring into **Lingmell Gill**.

Where the path splits as the **Brown Tongue** ridge begins to flatten out, take the left fork. This leads to the well-worn trail below **Pikes Crag**, and onto the northwest ridge, winding up to a large cairn on the lip of the summit plateau.

7 The right branch at the top of **Brown Tongue** leads up to a quite breath-taking intimacy with Scafell Crag on the way to **Mickledore**. Once on the narrow neck of ridge connecting the two great Scafells, turn left, passing the Mountain Rescue stretcher box. The path to the summit remains clear. For a brief diversion, once onto the plateau, bear half-left and, with modest effort and a hint of bravery, clamber onto the top of Pulpit Rock. A cairn marks the spot. From here you can enjoy a jealously guarded and airy new angle on Scafell Crag.

Ascent from Brotherilkeld 25 *off map S* or Wha House 26 *off map S*

There are two approaches to Cam Spout and then three choices thereafter – direct and scrambly up via Mickledore or looping round via Broadcrag Col (9 and 10).

Pikes Crag from below

Via Mickledore →*8.5km/5½ miles* ↑*1050m/3450ft* ⏱*5hr*
8 The speedier route to Cam Spout is via the Cowcove zig-zags. Embark either along the farm track from Wha House direct to Taw House, or take the farm-track from Brotherilkeld from the old red

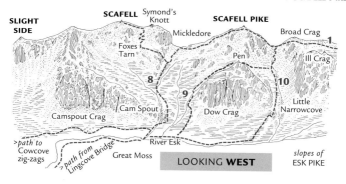

SLIGHT SIDE   SCAFELL   Symond's Knott   SCAFELL PIKE   Broad Crag   **1**

Mickledore

Foxes Tarn

Pen   Ill Crag

8   **10**

9

Cam Spout   Dow Crag   Little Narrowcove

Camspout Crag

>path to Cowcove zig-zags   path from Lingcove Bridge   River Esk   Great Moss   **LOOKING WEST**   slopes of ESK PIKE

telephone box, guided left of Brotherilkeld farmyard to a hand-gate, and, a matter of a few metres on, go left, crossing the wooden footbridge spanning the wonderfully tree-shaded **River Esk**. Traverse the pasture, with a wall right, to a ladder-stile entering the farmyard at Taw House.

Leave the farmyard by the gate at its northern end and follow the lane to a gate, thereafter on an open track, via two gateways, to a gate/ladder-stile below a ladder-stile at a sheepfold. A clear track continues to Scale Bridge, crossing the embowered cascades of Scale Gill. Ignore the direct path up from the bridge, and take the footpath signed further up the track. Watch for the acute turn left up through the bracken. (The path is clear enough.) Higher, the zig-zags afford a view into the Cowcove Beck ravine laced with birch and rowan, before entering the first of two marshy hollows. Keep to the dry western edge, crossing a plank over Damas Dubs. The path, well-evidenced underfoot, leads into the Esk catchment and meets up indistinctly with the west-side path. It then leads through a multi-penned sheepfold, curving round a low spur, littered with huge erratics, known as **Sampson's Stones**, set beneath the massive cliff of Camspout Crag. Keeping to the fringe of **Great Moss** marsh, the path now bears up half-left to reach the foot of **Cam Spout**.

9 Alternatively, the main valley approach holds tight to the Esk beside a fence. A clear path leads, via a gate in a wall, continuing to a ladder-stile beside a gate and small fold, where a path that began above the cattle grid at the foot of the Hardknott road converges. The valley soon narrows with three great cliffs catching the eye – Yew Crag up to the right on Hard Knott, and Brock Crag and Heron Crag to the left. The undulating path becomes smoother as it reaches the sheep-wash fold at the elegant single-span Lingcove Bridge.

The lower mare's tail of Cam Spout the path scrambles up the slabs to the right

From here Eskdale Needle (aka The Steeple) to the south takes on the appearance of a Roman thumbs-up. Cross the bridge and follow the path up Throstle Garth. As the mass of **Throstlehow Crag** is left behind we see the river taking wide meandering sweeps through a landscape reminiscent of a remote Highland glen, the path keeping close under Scar Lathing. As the vast amphitheatre surrounding **Great Moss** takes centre stage, see a turf-topped wall close right. This is the remnant of a medieval deer compound built by the monks of Furness Abbey. Wet marsh is unavoidable, but once the Esk shallows are forded the sponge is less of a problem trending northwest to the foot of **Cam Spout**, the most handsome of pencil-thin waterfalls.

Clamber up the bare rocks to the right of Cam Spout, ascending the increasingly rough combe above you, beneath Scafell's East Buttress. There is a path all the way, though it is inevitably loose nearing the saddle. From **Mickledore** head up the southwest ridge with Route **7** to reach the summit.

Via Little Narrowcove →8.7km/5½ miles ↑920m/3020ft ⏱5hr 30min

Arguably the most impressive of Scafell Pike's chest of crags is Esk Buttress (Dow Crag), the Central Pillar face commanding upper Eskdale. It is quirkily surmounted by a pimple of banded rock bearing a distinctly Celtic name, Pen. The route to this fabulous little top is arduous and largely pathless, but the summit well rewards the effort.

10 Bearing off right from Route **9**, a path contours along the edge of **Great Moss** and, after fording two gills, it is time to bend to the ascent. The rigg tapers to a gill to the left of **Dow Crag**. A worn path materialises, the climbers' descent route off the back of the crag. Don't be drawn into the gully, but keep on the steep rigg. As the slope gradually eases drift right to scramble to the top of **Pen**. There is a cairn and cause for much inner revelry at reaching this less than orthodox viewpoint. Ill Crag's stunning southern buttress simply steeples even from this elevated spot. Briefly follow the spine of the ridge, then work round to the left to find the breach in the ridge. A sheep path leads easily through into **Little Narrowcove**.

11 The direct route into Little Narrowcove does not hug the outflowing beck. To find the point of entry continue beside the infant **Esk**. After a large cairn, angle up the rigg left. A path emerges on approaching a gully. Clamber up, exiting right then left on a path drawing up beside Little Narrowcove Beck. The rarely seen beauties of this secret corrie deserve to be savoured. The final stages of the ascent zig-zag up the scree at the head to reach **Broadcrag Col**. It's a feather in your cap to have made this point by this means. Walkers converge here from Esk Hause and up the combe from the Corridor Route, but precious few from Little Narrowcove! Turn left, SW, for the summit.

The summit

A domed plateau well blessed with boulders and a few precious grassy patches culminates in a sturdy circular drystone-walled platform, which displaced the Ordnance Survey from the actual crown of the fell. All summits with loose rock seem to attract windbreak-makers and Scafell Pike is no exception. There are several of the normal, tumbledown type and one, situated towards the eastern brink, which lacks only a roof. I recommend visitors make the effort to wander around the plateau edge and enjoy some stunning new perspectives, the pick of the bunch that from above Dropping Crag.

Safe descents

For all its many year-round visitors, in nasty weather there can be no lonelier place than the summit of Scafell Pike. And once you've made it there, getting back is an altogether different proposition. Psychologically, the energy that drove you ever upward disappears in the instant you turn back, you may be tired and objectives are downbeat. Great Langdale, for instance, lies to the east, smack into the teeth of winter winds. Wasdale Head, by contrast, catches the prevailing ocean-borne breeze, by definition warmer, if potentially no less fierce.

For Wasdale Head (4km): start from the extra large cairn on the plateau edge 250m W of the summit. Descend the cairned path down the NW ridge

(**6**). Short of Lingmell Col the path veers left down into Hollow Stones, drawn naturally onto Brown Tongue and then into close company with Lingmell Gill.

For Seathwaite (6.5km): instead of veering left, go right, off the NW ridge, following the Corridor Route NE to Styhead Pass (**2**). From the stretcher box the old bridleway leads unerringly down to Stockley Bridge.

The return routes to Great Langdale (**1**) and Eskdale (**8**) are altogether rougher and longer. In bad weather either don't embark on these routes in the first place or if conditions unexpectedly close in turn down to Wasdale Head or Borrowdale.

Ridge routes

Great End →2.5km/1½ miles ↓185m/600ft ↑100m/330ft ⏲40min
Descend N via the narrow sorely eroded arête into the tight neck of Broadcrag Col. Traverse the ensuing bouldery shoulder into Illcrag Col, sweep up the gravel slope to a short boulder section over a crest and then down onto the broad saddle. Divert half-left, off the popular path to Esk Hause which leads down Calf Cove, and keep on the easy ground on the ridge heading N to a choice of two summit cairns.

Scafell →2km/1¼ miles ↓290m/950ft ↑275m/900ft ⏲1hr 20min
Aim SE to pick up a cairned path leading to the narrow connecting ridge of Mickledore and passing the stretcher box. The drama of Scafell wonderfully apparent, Broad Stand blocks off the ridge-end to walkers. Descend left into the combe beneath Scafell's East Buttress. Find the easy gully to the right (there is only one) and climb it to Foxes Tarn. Then tackle the partially restored zig-zag path climbing up onto the saddle and go left to the summit.

Lingmell →1.6km/1 mile ↓255m/840ft ↑85m/280ft ⏲45min
Walk NW across the boulder-field on the popular Wasdale path sprinkled with minor cairns. A larger cairn marks the scarp edge. From here wind down aiming for the depression, avoiding the natural urge to follow the stronger paths which veer left for Hollow Stones and right for the Corridor Route. Crossing the broken wall in the Lingmell Col depression rise NNW to the thrilling summit.

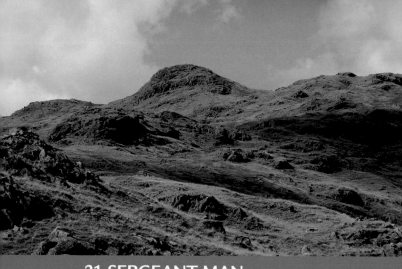

21 SERGEANT MAN 736M/2414FT

Climb it from	Stickle Ghyll **17** or Grasmere **6–9**
Character	Plateau-edge crest and a great focal point on the long ridge up from Silver How
Fell-friendly route	3
Summit grid ref	NY 286 089
Link it with	Blea Rigg, High Raise or Thunacar Knott
Part of	The Easedale Skyline

Just as Pavey Ark is the most striking feature of Thunacar Knott, so the unusual stack-like summit of Sergeant Man gives the basic plateau structure of High Raise its distinctive character. This ever-present landmark on horizons from all points of the compass marks the umbilical ridge connection with Easedale and its waters drain into Wythburn, Easedale and Great Langdale.

This little summit makes a superb objective for a fell walk from any of the surrounding valleys. No route is dull. How could they be in such marvellous surroundings?

For all its distance from a main valley base, you can climb the fell as a single summit via Stickle Ghyll (1), or the drama of Whitegill Crag (2), from Great

↑ Eastern aspect of Sergeant Man up the ridge   183

Langdale. From Grasmere you can climb onto the ridge via Silver How and Blea Rigg, or trek up Easedale via Belles Knott (3) or even Far Easedale, approaching from the top of Codale Head (4).

Ascent from Stickle Ghyll 17

A cluster of routes inevitably present themselves from this hugely popular walking base in Great Langdale. Choose Route 1 for the direct route and Route 2 for a more graded approach.

Via Stickle Ghyll →*4km/2½ miles*
↑*655m/2150ft* ⊙*2hr 40min*
1 Go either directly up the bridle-path from the hotel or ascend from Stickle Ghyll car park information shelter. The paths meet up by the fence-gap and follow the paved path beside **Stickle Ghyll**. Cross the footbridge and rise to a stile. Keep to the right-hand side of the valley, winding through a fenced area shielding the slope from erosion. The fencing has been compromised by sheep, thus minimising any benefits of relief from grazing.

The path forks, with pitching on both right and left paths. The popular route keeps left above the gill. Higher up, after mounting a rock-step this path fords the gill and arrives at the dam before **Stickle Tarn**.

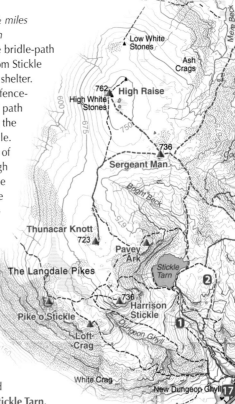

The right-hand variant path zig-zags as a stone stair to a further fork, where it bears up left and climbs over the shoulder of the intermediate outcrop below **Tarn Crag**, thereby linking with the Stickle Ghyll path and completing the ascent to the tarn.

(**2** If you carry straight on from the zig-zags to follow a turf trail to the right of Tarn Crag instead, you pass a ruined shelter and a walled enclosure to reach a feeder-gill at the eastern end of Stickle Tarn. Turn right here to follow a well-cairned path which curves round a marsh and rises easily northeastward

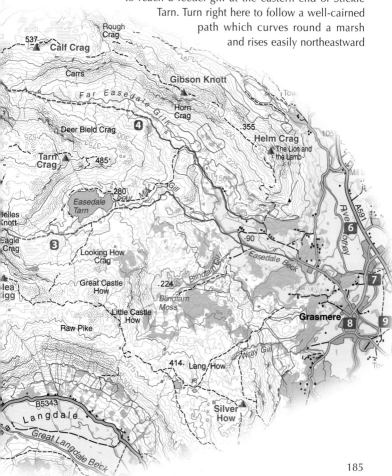

HIGH RAISE
SERGEANT MAN   Codale Head
THUNACAR KNOTT
TARN CRAG
PAVEY ARK
BLEA RIGG
1
HARRISON STICKLE
Stickle Tarn
2
Tarn Crag
Dungeon Ghyll
slopes of LOFT CRAG
Whitegill Crag

LOOKING **NORTH**

White Gill

Scout Crag

Great Langdale

Old Dungeon Ghyll Hotel *and* Blea Tarn

17

CHAPEL STILE

1

onto the **Blea Rigg** ridge, where you can turn left to follow the ridge to your destination.)

For the direct route, from the tarn follow the east shore path round to meet and follow **Bright Beck**, with Sergeant Man clearly in view ahead. Coming level with the steeply rising east ridge of **Pavey Ark**, a tangible path trends up a narrow defile due north beside a tributary gill, though the path becomes less

Codale Tarn

convincing higher up as the route naturally merges with the ridge rising to the summit. As the ridge is gained a lower path may be spotted, traversing below the fell-top from the great slab to the head of Bright Beck – possibly a hasty short-cut to avoid Sergeant Man. Follow the ridge path up to the summit.

Ascent from Grasmere 6–9

Natural routes lead up the ridges of Blea Rigg and Tarn Crag (described as ridge routes elsewhere) but these two dale approaches make excellent alternatives.

Via Easedale Tarn →5.5km/3½ miles ↑685m/2245ft ⏱3hr

3 The popular path to Easedale Tarn leaves the Easedale Road via the footbridge opposite Oak Lodge, traversing meadows via gates. Much of the way is paved. The path winds up beside **Sour Milk Gill**, the excited waters churning down frenzied falls. Conical drumlins on either side of **Easedale Tarn** emphasise the glacial origins of this bleak amphitheatre. The conical top of Tarn Crag looms close right, while Blea Rigg forms the southern sidewall.

The old path continues along the southern side of the tarn and its main feedergill, and has several stepped sections beside steep cascades. Up to the right the arresting **Belles Knott** looks like a good climb for scramblers, but

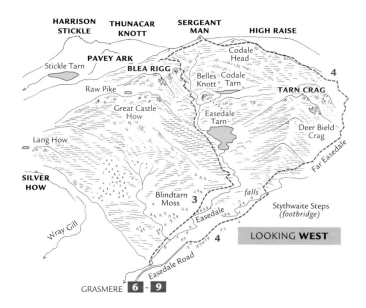

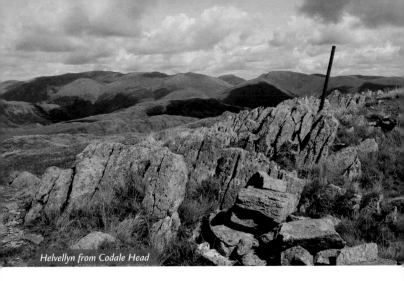

Helvellyn from Codale Head

once you get above the falls the knott soon shows itself to be a sham. A side-path bears right, fording the gill, to visit the hanging waters of **Codale Tarn**, with its tiny outflow and picturesque isle set beneath the great slope of Codale Head. Keep with the main path which zig-zags up to a ridge-top path interchange west of Blea Rigg. Turn right and mount the rocky ridge to the northwest for the very first glimpse of the fell-top. Two early path options reunite at the giant slab, and a solitary path continues to ford the outflow of a marsh and then climbs the distinctive summit knoll beyond.

Via Far Easedale →*6km/3¾ miles* ↑*685m/2245ft* ⏱*3hr 15min*

4 The old pony path up **Far Easedale** provides an enjoyable alternative, and is signposted 'Greenup Edge' from the Easedale Road-end. Proceed via the **Stythwaite Steps** footbridge to the saddle at the very top of the dale. Follow the metal stakes of the old Cumberland–Westmorland county-boundary fence left over Broadstone Head and on to **Codale Head** at which point the summit comes into view. Continue to claim the top.

The summit

The summit is not quite the bold stack of Pike o'Stickle, rather a kid-brother of similarly resilient rock. Fellwalkers instinctively love this high place, for all that the bare outcrop has but a bedraggled cairn as monument to the many thousands of appreciative visitations. Note the old Ordnance Survey benchmark on the very top, dating from the survey of 1860, almost obscured by wear.

Northern aspect with Bowfell directly behind the summit

Safe descents

Being the lynch-pin off High Raise for Great Langdale via Bright Beck and Stickle Ghyll (**1**) and Grasmere via Easedale Tarn (**3**), the clear path leading SE down the ridge is a reliable guide in doubtful conditions.

Ridge routes

Blea Rigg →2km/1¼ miles ↓205m/670ft ↑15m/50ft ⊕40min
The ridge path descending SE is well marked and supported with cairns. The slope eases at a meeting of paths, which marks the transition to the broader ridge of Blea Rigg. Weave by a rock pool and skirt three distinct rock knolls to reach the summit, distinguished by its tiny cairn perched on a chunky rock.

High Raise →0.8km/½ mile ↓10m/35ft ↑30m/100ft ⊕20min
Head NW, passing pools in crossing the open plateau. Skirt the old fence-corner by even larger pools to reach the summit with its jumble of rocks, wind-shelter and Ordnance Survey pillar.

Thunacar Knott →1.6km/1 mile ↓60m/200ft ↑45m/150ft ⊕35min
Head W. The going is easy underfoot, and a clear path on the ground leads to a wide shallow depression at the head of Bright Beck. Here join the prominent ridge path from High Raise heading S. As the first rocks are encountered on the easy rise, bear off half-right from the main trail to reach the summit cairn.

22 SILVER HOW 395M/1296FT

Climb it from	Stickle Ghyll **17**, Elterwater **16**, High Close **15** or Grasmere **6–9**
Character	Peerless viewpoint overlooking the sylvan Vale of Grasmere
Fell-friendly route	10
Summit grid ref	NY 325 066
Link it with	Blea Rigg or Loughrigg Fell
Part of	The Easedale Skyline

Silver How has an elegant profile so definitive of the Grasmere fellscape, forming a backdrop to sylvan views across the lake, that many walkers feel drawn to conquer its summit. But appearance is deceptive. This fell is nothing more than the scarp-end of a broad ridge leading up towards Blea Rigg and the Langdale Pikes. Another northwesterly ridge rises up to it from the top of the Redbank Road over Dow Bank and Spedding Crag to where, as Meg's Gill slices into the fell, it rises smartly again flaring towards the north and the tip of this prominent craggy escarpment.

Many ridge walkers bypass the summit of Silver How but this classic Grasmere viewpoint does make a worthy end in itself and you can be sure that

↑ *Silver How from Dow Bank (photo: Don Dawber)*

Wordsworth stood here before you, taking inspiration from the village as well as the high fells. The ridge to Castle How is a grand scenic parade with numerous undulations to intrigue the wanderer, with nothing much more than sheep trods to follow in places.

Routes to the top are varied and plentiful, and all are worthy – made the more so by the scenic virtues of the ultimate objective. There are seven prime routes from the Langdale side (1–7), six from Grasmere (9–14) and one from the pass in between (8)!

Ascent from Stickle Ghyll 17

This route is more often used in descent, but makes an excellent approach to the Silver How ridge, especially for views back towards the stunning surround of majestic fells.

Via Pye Howe →2km/1¼ miles ↑305m/1000ft ⏲1hr

1 Just over a kilometre east along the road from the New Dungeon Ghyll, a footpath embarks from the valley road midway between Pye Howe and the Long House.

A kissing-gate gives entry into a pasture, where you initially keep the wall to the left. Ascend with half-a-dozen waymark posts as aids and cross broken intermediate walls. Much mature scrub colonises the enclosures. A ladder-stile crosses the intake wall at the top, and the path, at first stony, becomes a

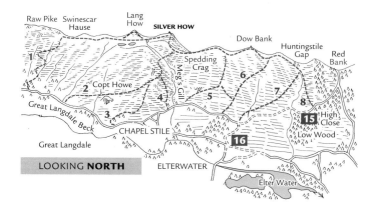

pleasant turf trail, beyond the solitary, gill-shading holly. Wind steadily to the ridge-top at **Swinescar Hause**, joining the ridge path heading right (southeast).

Before the group of three tarns known as Youdell Tarn take the opportunity to include **Lang How** (some 19m, 62ft, higher than Silver How) – scant trace of a path leads up onto its grassy ridge, and a cairn gives reason to pause before the path winds down the southern slope to rejoin the ridge path. Traverse the headstream of **Wray Gill** direct to the summit.

Ascent from Elterwater 16

To get to Chapel Stile from Elterwater take the Langdale Rambler bus in season or stroll into the village from Elterwater on the road or beside Great Langdale Beck. In Meg's Gill, a stunning re-entrant

Youdell Tarn

ravine, the village has an irresistible climb, which the first three routes described here make the most of.

Via Copt Howe
→ *2km/1¼ miles*
↑ *305m/1000ft*
🕐 *1hr 10min*
2 A matter of 100m east of Harry Place Farm, opposite a roadside barn, a footpath is discreetly signposted. The path climbs the bank to a stile in a wall-linking fence. Ascend with the wall to the right and join a green track going right. Cross the saddle behind **Copt Howe**. The path traverses the rough slopes,

taking one notable
rocky step up during its
approach to **Meg's Gill**. This top
path can be joined from three other paths

Lang How

ascending from the village and goes on to meet Route **4** on its way to the summit.

3 One path begins about 700m further east than Route 2, in **Chapel Stile** and just past a big bend in the road. A footpath is signed from a gate that leads to a stile and an awkward descent through the old Thrang Quarry. Just before entering a lane – another access point from the village street west of Holy Trinity Church – bear up left between the retaining walls in the quarry to mount the ridge with a gill to the left. The path forks. Both ways meet the **Copt Howe** path (**2**) but the right-hand one is the better option.

Via Meg's Gill →*1.5km/1 mile* ↑*305m/1000ft* ⏱*1hr*

4 A further path leaves the road east of the church and before Walthwaite Lodge. Climb the bank, with the wall to the right, on a narrow path through the bracken. Rounding the wall on the brow, ascend on the west side of the **Meg's Gill** ravine, rising to meet the top path (Route **2**).

Now continue up the gill to a high ford, and contour with a fine view down and across to a waterfall below the ford. Finally rise onto the ridge, precisely where the Silver How escarpment imposes itself on the lesser ridge from **High Close**. Trend left to the summit.

Via Dow Bank →*2km/1¼ miles* ↑*305m/1000ft* ⏱*1hr 10min*

5 Other paths leading up from the road leading from Chapel Stile to Grasmere over Red Bank include the route onto the **Spedding Crag** to **Dow Bank** saddle beginning just east of **Meg's Gill** and Speddy Cottage. Pass through a hand-gate and ascend with a wall on the right. Up to the left see Raven Crag, a popular evening haunt for climbers. Rise to a turning point where the path switches left and leads straight up to the saddle. Follow the switch-back course over Spedding Crag until a more significant step in the ridge occurs. Take the rising line by a large cairn, angling right for the scarp-top summit.

   6 A bit further along the road a turf path bears off half-left for 150m, then turns directly uphill through the bracken. A strong sheep path may be followed to the left, contouring to the turning point on the path up from Speddy Cottage (to join Route **5**), or you can simply keep going up to the cairn on **Dow Crag** and on down to the saddle to join Route **5** there.

   7 From the open common above the Walthwaite Bottom car park several paths leave the road for the **Huntingstile Gap**. The first is the primary route, and departs some few metres right of the steep road junction (200m on from the start of Route **6**). An early branch left climbs onto the **Dow Bank** ridge, while the main thrust of the path takes a steady line, passing an electricity compound to reach the deep gap. (This is also a popular route over to Grasmere, which later descends as a cobbled lane to the Redbank Road at Lea Cottage.) Turn left here to join the ridge path over to Dow Bank and Route **6**.

Ascent from High Close 15

Via Dow Bank →*2km/1¼ miles* ↑*300m/990ft* ⏱*1hr*

8 Various impromptu paths also leave the open road west of High Close Youth Hostel, again gathering in **Huntingstile Gap** in readiness to mount the **Dow Bank** ridge (following Route **7**).

Ascent from Grasmere 6–9

Choose from two popular paths from the village centre (Routes 9 and 11), with a rough cross-country link between them (Route 12), and a surreptitious approach from the north on indistinct paths (Route 10).

Via **Wray Gill** → *1.5km/1 mile* ↑*330m/1085ft* ⏱*50min*

9 From the middle of Grasmere village, at the junction of Broadgate with Langdale Road, take the road leading northwest. Enter the parkland environs of Allan Bank. Keep right on the approach drive to reach the cottages and enter a narrow gated lane. (This point can be reached from Easedale Road, via Goody Bridge Cottages, where a footpath leads over stepping-stones, via hand-gates, and up a pasture to cross a drive that rises to a fence-stile into the lane above the cottages.) The lane duly emerges at a kissing-gate onto the open fell. The path climbs initially with a wall close left and rises through juniper. Watch for the path forking left to a ford of **Wray Gill**. This is the direct line to the fell summit, while the right path wanders onto the ridge under **Lang How**.

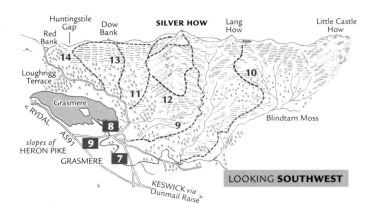

LOOKING **SOUTHWEST**

Via **Blindtarn Moss** → *2.5km/1½ miles* ↑*330m/1085ft* ⏱*1hr 25min*

10 Follow Easedale Road and cross Easedale Beck via the footbridge at Oak Lodge. Advance along the roughly cobbled path, which soon runs with a wall to the left and the beck to the right. After the restored New Bridge watch for the yellow waymark on the gate to the left. The path guides, via a meadow, to a metal gate and through light woodland to join, at another gate, the track leading to a pair of holiday cottages. Pass on by the white railings to a wooden gate in the field corner. Continue with the wall on the left, the route jostling

Grasmere from the summit

with the gill as it ascends to a waymark post directing right, below a gate with a 'private' notice. Dense bracken is replaced by juniper at the open hollow of **Blindtarn Moss**. The path forks – take the more minor left-hand path. After a small ford the indistinct path continues up the wet slope through juniper and rushes. The fell eases and a sheep path materialises, drawing up to the skyline and the ridge path. Turn left and pass three pools beneath **Lang How**, known as Youdell Tarn. At the third tarn take the right-hand fork path bound for Silver How, now clearly in view ahead, joining the last stages of Route **1**.

Via Kelbarrow →*2.5km/1½ miles* ↑*305m/1000ft* ⏱*1hr 15min*
11 From the entrance to Redbank Road car park follow the road left. At the drive entrance to Kelbarrow, opposite the Faeryland boat hire/tearoom, go right, up the walled lane. Ascend via two kissing-gates, now under the rough slope of the fell, and the path keeps the intake wall close left. (**12** Should you relish a spot of rough-stuff walking, you may consider branching right as the path first levels. A sheep path contours across the scree and bracken slope, becoming less definite as you come high above the open-pasture section of

the approach. Climb to the skyline well before the craggy ravine of **Wray Gill** and follow the scarp top (there is no path). The views of the lake and over the village to Great Rigg and Fairfield are exceptional.) Otherwise continue to the wall corner and either ascend the eroded gully direct to the summit or continue, via two fords, to the ridge-top path interchange. Turn right, mounting via a large cairn, and keep right along the scarp brow to the summit.

Via Dow Bank →*3.2km/2 miles* ↑*320m/1050ft* ⏱*1hr 40min*

Two more routes lead off from further up the ever-busy Redbank Road.

13 For a more sylvan option, though with hampered views, continue with Redbank Road to turn right into the drive leading to the Wyke. The fenced drive passes between stately oaks. At a gill crossing, with the house in view, turn right, slipping over the higher bridge. Go via the remains of a metal kissing-gate, and embark upon a path which rises as a stony trail through light birch wood to reach a wall-stile and hand-gate onto the fell. Either continue through the scrub and bracken onto **Dow Bank** to turn right with the ridge path (Route **6**), or go right, with the wall to the right, via marshy patches, to the curving wall corner and ascend the gully direct.

    14 Another path leaves the Redbank Road further up opposite **The Lea**. Initially rising as a drive to Huntingstile House, this becomes a cobbled lane to a hand-gate then rises to the **Huntingstile Gap** where you can join Route **7** to follow the undulations of the ridge path to the summit. (Alternatively, take the metal gate, immediately left of the hand-gate, to join a lovely woodland parade which rejoins Redbank Road opposite the path to **Loughrigg Terrace**. At this point a path steps off the road and goes up three immediate steps to curve round, via a hand-gate, into Huntingstile Gap.)

The summit

A tumbled wreck of a cairn sits on the bare top surveying the luxuriant Grasmere vale. The all-round view is most rewarding. Visitors can train their eyes both on the detail within the vale, of village, meadow, woods and lake, and on the lovely surround of higher fells. So although it is not the highest point upon the near mass of fell, Lang How having that status, it is the natural viewpoint.

Safe descents

The eastern slope of the fell is lined with crags, so all descents need to begin from the depression some 100m west-southwest from the cairn. The path leading N, fording Wray Gill and bound for Allan Bank (**9**), is the best in poor visibility. To the S find assurance in the ridge path leading SE that reaches the unenclosed Elterwater to High Close road off Dow Bank (**8**).

Ridge routes

Blea Rigg →*3.2km/2 miles* ↓*45m/150ft* ↑*205m/670ft* ⏲*1hr*
The path leads off WNW, passing below Lang How, superior to Silver How by 19m (62ft). Pass two pools hosting bogbean and continue over the brow to a much larger tarn, where reed encroachment is so advanced that it has the least open water of the three. The path weaves easily along the ridge to the marshy hollow of Swinescar Hause, from where the line of least resistance trends diagonally across the slope by a curious low shelter to traverse Castle How. Fellwanderers may choose to head up from the sheepfold (pathless) to reach the top of Raw Pike (no cairn) or the southern top of Great Castle How, with its fine view of Blea Rigg ahead. These routes reunite at the quartz stones and pass pools en route to the summit.

Loughrigg Fell →*4km/2½ miles* ↓*290m/950ft* ↑*230m/750ft* ⏲*1hr 15min*
Leave the scarp-top summit, angling left to a large cairn, from where the ridge path pitches purposefully downhill. From the foot of this initial bank a sequence of switch-backs is crossed via Spedding Crag and Dow Bank. Reaching Huntingstile Gap bear left via a hand-gate in a fence, and the path curves right via steps onto the Redbank Road – watch for traffic. Turn right and take the first left, descending through a gate onto the W end of Loughrigg Terrace. Climb the prominent path southeast via the Grasmere cairn to reach the summit.

23 STEEL FELL 553M/1814FT

Climb it from	Mill Bridge **5**, Dunmail Raise **4** and Steel End **3**
Character	A simple ridge between Thirlmere and Grasmere standing guard over Dunmail Raise
Fell-friendly route	1
Summit grid ref	NY 319 112
Link it with	Calf Crag
Part of	The Greenburn Horseshoe

Steel Fell is a triangle of sturdy fell defined by Greenburn Dale, Wythburn Dale and Dunmail Raise. Being so distantly connected to Calf Crag lends it a certain dignity for standing alone between such giants of central Lakeland but also makes it an appealingly accessible half-day challenge.

This is a lovely little fell to climb and, overlooking Dunmail Raise and set upon the Lakeland watershed, its situation lends it quite some distinction as a viewpoint. Grand is the huge whaleback western aspect of the Helvellyn range and charming the long view up Thirlmere to Blencathra. Elsewhere see the Coniston fells in a tight huddle and the massive bulk of fell at the core of the Central Fells rising to High Raise and, much nearer, the broad mass of Ullscarf,

↑ *The summit of Steel Fell (also known as Dead Pike) from Gibson Knott* enhanced when shafts of sunlight play on the near buttresses of Nab and Castle Crags.

Ascents lead up from Grasmere (1), Dunmail Raise (2–3), Steel End (4) and Wythburn (5–6) and can be easily combined into circular tours for a slightly longer expedition.

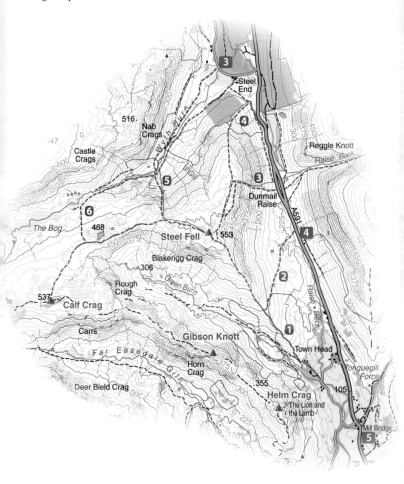

Ascent from Mill Bridge 5

Take time to admire the views from this classic route.

Direct → *2.5km/1½ miles* ↑*475m/1560ft* ⏱*1hr 15min*

1 Follow the road down to Low Mill Bridge, crossing the Rothay, then turn right, and directly after **Ghyll Foot** bear left up the 'private driveway' via a pair of cattle grids to pass the tree-screened Helmside. Go through the gate beyond Turn Howe and keep right, rising to a gate at a wall junction. A clear path rises up the pasture to a kissing-gate and gains access to the open fell. Ahead the southeast ridge climbs by steady, stepped stages. En route take time to admire the view back to Helm Crag and the wilds of truncated Greenburn Dale. The higher you get the more impressive Seat Sandal looks. Approaching the summit the path forks. The east-top cairn catches the eye first, but both paths weave by shallow pools to the ultimate cairn.

Ascent from Dunmail Raise 4

Via Cotra → *2.7km/1¾ miles* ↑*320m/1050ft* ⏱*1hr 30min*

A cross-country line straight up from the Dunmail Raise parking spot

2 A useful optional route onto the southeast ridge begins from the ladder-stile opposite the **Achille Ratti Hut** layby. A pathless line is followed that fords the diminished **Raise Beck**, severed from its upper section by the construction of the Thirlmere reservoir, which diverted the headstream into the reservoir. Cross the **Cotra** moraine keeping right of the feeder beck running down the slope, encountering bracken on the rise, and bending left to contour just above the enclosure wall to the skyline ridge. On the ridge turn right to join Route **1**.

Direct →*0.8km/½ mile* ↑*305m/1000ft* ⏱*30min*

Gird your loins and steel yourself for this one, though there is actually nothing out of the ordinary about this quick climb.

3 Walk a kilometre up the pass from the layby, keeping to the left-hand kerb of the northbound carriageway when the road splits, to find the ladder-stile at the summit. Set off over this in a westerly direction to climb the pasture slope that drifts towards the gill and boundary fence. As a finger of scree reaches down, slip over the gill and, keeping the fence tight right, climb the steep final section to the top. Take a breather and gaze over the gulf of Dunmail Raise into the impressive ravine of Raise Beck, sliced into the Helvellyn massif as if struck by a massive lumberjack's axe. Either follow the sheep trod along the edge of **Ash Crags** or keep to the ridge path that runs closer to the fence (a sensible precaution on gusty days) and leads to the summit at the fence-corner.

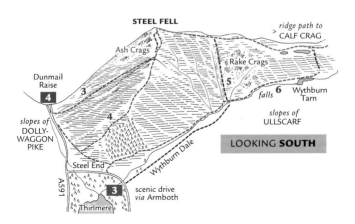

Ascent from Steel End 3

Three routes can be contemplated from this northern base.

Direct → 1.5km/1 mile ↑375m/1230ft ⏱1hr

4 The principal route is the north ridge. Leave the Steel End car park and turn left. Follow the road to just short of the entrance to West Head Farm. A sign directs to the right at the beginning of the newly surfaced bridle-path to **Dunmail Raise**. Pass up by the cottages and subsequent farm-house and follow a short lane leading to a gate. Ignore the obvious gravel

Dunmail Raise from Ash Crags

track to the right, and instead keep the wall close right along the cycle path. Pass through a gate, then leave the new recreational route. Head up the bank and come above the plantation to reach a hand-gate where a wall straps the ridge. This is a good moment to look across the valley to Birkside Gill, draining Nethermost and Dollywaggon Pikes.

The north ridge climbs steadily on, a grassy plod relieved only by pauses to look back down the length of Thirlmere. The grassy ridge relents to a gentler gradient on the broadening upper ridge, and leads by a metal stake on a knoll to a stile in the right-angle of the boundary fence. From here the fence makes the awful drop directly to Dunmail Raise, making this edge a fine spot to gaze down on the ancient cairn in the pass, as well as up the facing Raise Beck to Cofa Pike and Fairfield. Continue on with Route **3**.

Via Rake Crags →2km/1¼ miles ↑380m/1250ft ⏱1hr 20min

Two ascents (Routes 5 and 6) can be considered out of upper Wythburn Dale. This first option will appeal to people a little less concerned about ease of travel and more intent on getting to the top.

5 From the Steel End car park go left the few metres to a kissing-gate or continue over the bridge a further few metres to a hand-gate and steps leading down into the meadow. The two paths advance in harmony either side of the fenced **Wyth Burn**, via gates, ladder-stiles and stiles, and reunite at a wooden footbridge.

Ascend beside the wall and fence adjacent to the minor gill due south. As a means of gaining the ridge, it is practical and safe, but oh so steep! Turn left at the top to follow the fence to the summit.

Via Wythburn Dale →3.5km/2¼ miles ↑390m/1280ft ⏱1hr 30min
6 For a more serene option, at the footbridge continue on the dale path that climbs above the southern bank of **Wyth Burn**. There are two fine waterslide cascades, which are all the more exciting when a strong wind drives spray back. Pass the twin portal moraines, anciently breached, that drain the lost **Wythburn Tarn**. Water nonetheless does tend to linger. It must love the place, as I suspect you will. Above, Castle Crags' overhanging buttresses catch the eye. Pass the sinuous vestigial tarn and branch off the clear path, climbing pathless to the left onto the ridge. Turn left to skirt right around the two large plateau-top tarns and to join the ridge path that leads unerringly east for a couple of kilometres to the summit.

The summit

This is a cracking viewpoint, with its principal cairn resting on a small plinth of reddish rock beside the remains of the old metal county-boundary fence. Some 100m due east, at a slightly lower elevation, a second cairn sits at the angle of the old metal fence.

The summit cairn

A more recent wooden fence switches upon the summit, taking a cleaner line north to the point, nearly two kilometres distant, where the pre-1974 Cumberland–Westmorland boundary fence plummets east to Dunmail Raise.

Safe descents

The N (**4**) and S (**1**) ridges are benign enough for a quick getaway in difficult conditions.

Ridge route

Calf Crag →*2.4km/1½ miles* ↓*90m/300ft* ↑*70m/230ft* ⊕*40min*
Walk W beside the fence with the occasional marshy hollow to straddle. The path dips as the fence departs north, and several knolls are avoided en route to a large marsh containing two innominate tarns. After this point the path is less well defined. It parts company with the intermittent metal boundary stakes as it sweeps SE over damp ground at the head of Greenburn Dale to rise to the prominent knoll-top of Calf Crag.

Plateau tarn on Steel Fell

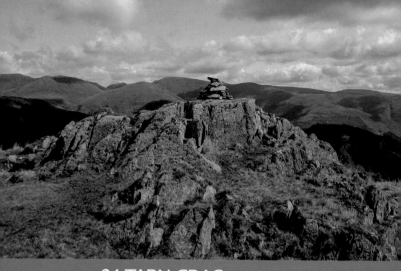

24 TARN CRAG 485M/1591FT

Climb it from	Grasmere 6–9
Character	Proud headland and worthy objective set between Easedale Tarn and Far Easedale
Fell-friendly route	4
Summit grid ref	NY 303 093
Link it with	Sergeant Man
Part of	The Easedale Skyline

Codale Head throws down ridges from the head of Easedale to embrace two chill-watered corries, Codale and Easedale Tarns. With Blea Rigg casting shadows from its southern brink, Tarn Crag basks in the sun to the north, and in turn shades Far Easedale. From the top of Sour Milk Gill, where many a tourist has stopped over the centuries to contemplate the lower, larger tarn, the domed top of Tarn Crag is the much-photographed backdrop, and hence its name. However, it is best appreciated from high on Calf Crag on the other side of Far Easedale, with Deer Bield and Ferngill Crags for foreground.

Easily reached from busy Grasmere in less than a couple of hours, the summit offers views of the Vale of Grasmere, or of the famous tarn, from different points,

↑ *Summit cairn on Tarn Crag*

and the summit ridge, running westwards, deserves to be relished for its own sake – the pools and rocks a wild garden to explore.

The fell can be conveniently climbed via its east ridge (1), or from either flank (Easedale, 2 or Far Easedale, 4–5) or a more circuitous route (3) takes in the lovely, lonely Codale Tarn and the pencil-point of Belles Knott.

Ascent from Grasmere 6–9

Via Easedale Tarn →3.5km/2¼ miles ↑425m/1395ft ◷1hr 30min

There's no way to avoid bushwhacking through bracken on the two most direct routes to the top.

1 Follow Easedale Road via **Goody Bridge** to cross the footbridge opposite Oak Lodge. A path leads via a hand-gate across a meadow, coming close to **Easedale Beck** with a wall close left. Ignore the inviting New Bridge to the right. From a gate cross **Blindtarn Gill** bridge. Ignore the track to Brimmer Head Farm on the right and

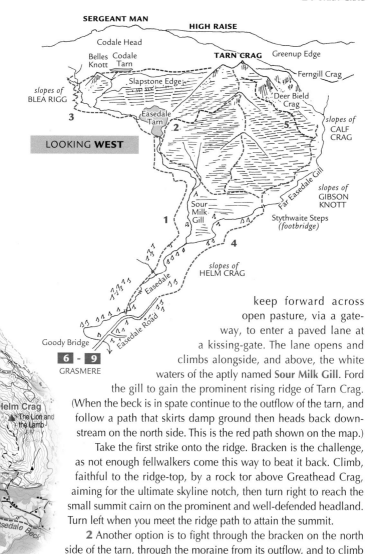

SERGEANT MAN

HIGH RAISE

Codale Head

Belles Codale
Knott Tarn

TARN CRAG Greenup Edge

Ferngill Crag

slopes of
BLEA RIGG

Slapstone Edge

Deer Bield
Crag

3

Easedale
Tarn

2

slopes of
CALF
CRAG

5

LOOKING **WEST**

Far Easedale Gill

Sour
Milk
Gill

slopes of
GIBSON
KNOTT

1

Stythwaite Steps
(footbridge)

4

slopes of
HELM CRAG

Easedale

Goody Bridge

6 - 9
GRASMERE

Easedale Road

Helm Crag
The Lion and
the Lamb

sedale Beck

keep forward across
open pasture, via a gate-
way, to enter a paved lane at
a kissing-gate. The lane opens and
climbs alongside, and above, the white
waters of the aptly named **Sour Milk Gill**. Ford
the gill to gain the prominent rising ridge of Tarn Crag.
(When the beck is in spate continue to the outflow of the tarn, and
follow a path that skirts damp ground then heads back downstream on the north side. This is the red path shown on the map.)

Take the first strike onto the ridge. Bracken is the challenge,
as not enough fellwalkers come this way to beat it back. Climb,
faithful to the ridge-top, by a rock tor above Greathead Crag,
aiming for the ultimate skyline notch, then turn right to reach the
small summit cairn on the prominent and well-defended headland.
Turn left when you meet the ridge path to attain the summit.

2 Another option is to fight through the bracken on the north
side of the tarn, through the moraine from its outflow, and to climb

209

Sour Milk Gill

an old shepherds' trod on an indistinct zig-zag onto the high ridge left of Greathead Crag.

Via Codale Tarn
→4.5km/2¾ miles
↑440m/1445ft ⏱1hr 50min

Anyone seeking to develop a circular tour including Tarn Crag would be wise to bring Codale Tarn into the equation.

3 Continue with the main path from the outflow of Easedale Tarn, running along the south side of the tarn to join the main feeder-gill below **Blea Rigg**. The path has been greatly improved, and in parts forms a stone staircase rising with the cascades, a scene enhanced by the spire-like presence of **Belles Knott**. A minor path forks right above the cascades, fords the gill, and climbs over the west shoulder of Belles Knott to reach **Codale Tarn**, a place of quiet retreat. The quaint rocky isle may tempt a few to try their luck at reaching it without wetting their socks! Pass the tiny outflow and climb the damp northern slope by a ruined sheepfold to join the ridge path, and turn right to the summit.

Via Far Easedale →3.7km/2¼ miles ↑425m/1395ft ⏱1hr 30min

The fell can be approached with equal alacrity from Far Easedale, beginning on the bridle-path popularised even further by Wainwright's Coast to Coast Walk. The second option here is a little wilder and involves some pathless boulder-hopping.

4 From the road-end at Easedale House follow the public bridleway signs indicating 'Far Easedale, Borrowdale'. This route advances to the **Stythwaite Steps** footbridge.

Deer Bield Crag

Cross the footbridge, and here you have a choice. The first option is to follow the path up by the wall, noting the massive boulder capped with luxuriant heather growth to the left, onto the ridge-end, thus linking to the path to **Easedale Tarn** and Routes **2** or **3**.

5 Alternatively, keep right from Stythwaite Steps footbridge on the clear path running up **Far Easedale**. Pass on by the naturally drained site of a tarn overlooked by Pike of Carrs. Try branching from the path to find a way up through the bracken in the vicinity of a gill. An apparent grass strip gives the illusion of an easy way, but keep eyes focused on the towering cliff of **Deer Bield**. There is no path, but the going is basically trouble-free, if tangly and wet. Near the base of the crag is a group of mighty boulders. Boulder hop – there is precious little scree – then either clamber straight onto the ridge or keep up to the right above the crag. Prolong contact with the eastern rim of the fell before you are finally forced to drift left to join the ridge path that rises up through the notch to the ultimate point.

The summit

The craggy top-knot is a thoroughly delightful place to visit, and from the small cairn you can enjoy a lovely view back towards the green Vale of Grasmere – the only thing lacking is Easedale Tarn itself. This deficiency is speedily remedied by going south,

Summit peak rising above the east ridge

back across the ridge path in the notch, some 100m, to stand beside a significantly larger and strategically placed cairn that commands a bird's-eye view down upon the glistening waters.

Safe descents

Stick to the ridge due E and at the foot go either left for the Stythwaite Steps footbridge (**4**) or right to ford Sour Milk Gill (leading to **1**).

Ridge route

Sergeant Man →*2km/1¼ miles* ↓*5m/15ft* ↑*255m/840ft* ⏱*50min*
A narrow ridge path weaves west along the marshy top amid glaciated rock outcrops. As the slope steepens, be careful not to catch your feet in peat holes caused by surface wash-out. The path ascends beside a gill to reach a cigar-shaped pool adorned with bogbean, then links up with the ridge path ascending Broadstone Head from the saddle at the top of Far Easedale. Follow the old county-boundary fence metal stakes on the left to Codale Head, rounding a marsh to reach the summit stake.

Easedale Tarn

212

25 THUNACAR KNOTT 723M/2372FT

Climb it from	Great Langdale **17** or Stonethwaite **2**
Character	Unassuming bristling brow behind the familiar summits of the Langdale Pikes
Fell-friendly route	1
Summit grid ref	NY 280 080
Link it with	Harrison Stickle, High Raise or Sergeant Man
Part of	The Langdale Pikes

Above the handsome face of Pavey Ark this fell is the natural crown, highbrow and aloof. The summit is no more than a gentle final swelling scattered with vertically fractured rock and a shallow pool, so modest that authoritative writers have frequently missed it as the true top.

This is, therefore, another top too often overlooked. Most fellwalkers hasten on to High Raise, Sergeant Man or the Pikes, brushing over the eastern shoulder, unaware that a separate fell is at hand. But it boasts a panorama of fells that would be the envy of many a lesser height.

If you do make it your objective, you're most likely to be coming up from Langdale, via Pike How (1) or Stickle Tarn (2) but for a more substantial excursion Borrowdale via Stake Beck (3) is also an option!

↑ *Summit of Thunacar Knott*

Ascent from Stickle Ghyll 17

Via Pike How or Stickle Ghyll →2.5km/1½ miles ↑650m/2135ft
⏱ 1hr 30min

Two paths lead up from Langdale. The one via Pike How (Route 1) is the one less travelled.

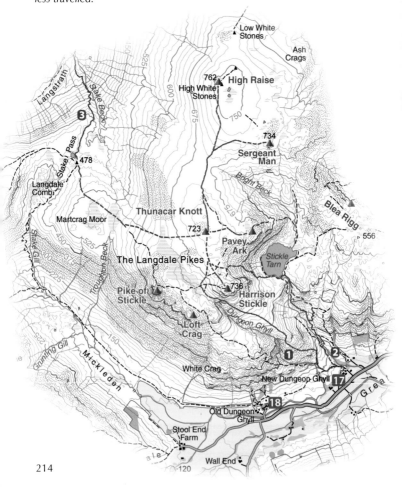

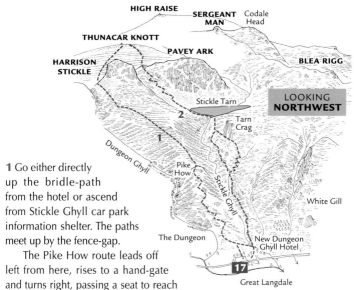

HIGH RAISE
SERGEANT MAN
Codale Head
THUNACAR KNOTT
PAVEY ARK
HARRISON STICKLE
BLEA RIGG
Stickle Tarn
LOOKING **NORTHWEST**
2
Tarn Crag
1
Dungeon Ghyll
Pike How
Stickle Ghyll
White Gill
The Dungeon
New Dungeon Ghyll Hotel
17
Great Langdale

1 Go either directly up the bridle-path from the hotel or ascend from Stickle Ghyll car park information shelter. The paths meet up by the fence-gap.

The Pike How route leads off left from here, rises to a hand-gate and turns right, passing a seat to reach a stile. Keep the wall on your right, and do not ford **Dungeon Ghyll**. The well-marked path bears left mounting the steep slope in steady stages. Much of it has been re-engineered to cope with the inevitable heavy foot traffic. Many walkers use this as their return leg after the ascent via Stickle Ghyll, though they would be better resorting to the Mark Gate path off **Loft Crag**, as it has the best base. Climbing up to the saddle behind **Pike How**, make the move right to stand on top. It is a super viewpoint.

The main path proceeds across the open pasture aiming west-northwest for the high shoulder above the deep upper gorge of Dungeon Ghyll. The aggressive slope beneath Harrison Crag affords the path little room, so take your time and watch your footing, as there is loose ground to negotiate. On entering Harrison Combe come to the path junction above the peat-hopping stepping-stones. Bear right to find the narrow trod rising due north out of the combe towards the summit.

2 The Stickle Ghyll route continues with the paved path from the fence-gap, leading up the popular trail to the tarn. Cross the footbridge and rise to a stile. Keep to the right-hand side of the valley, winding through a fenced area intended to shield the slope from erosion.

Vertically fissured plateau outcrop on Thunacar Knott

The path forks, with pitching on both right and left paths. The popular route keeps left above the gill. Higher up, after mounting a rock-step this path fords the gill and arrives at the dam before **Stickle Tarn**. The right-hand variant path zig-zags as a stone stair to a further fork, where it bears up left and climbs over the shoulder of the intermediate outcrop below **Tarn Crag**, thereby linking with the Stickle Ghyll path and completing the ascent to the tarn.

Ahead is the massive crag of Pavey Ark frowning down on the cool, dark waters of Stickle Tarn, and high to the left rises Harrison Stickle. Go left on the obvious path, which has received some restorative paving, though more is needed. Work up the slope to the right of the buttresses. On meeting the contouring path from Harrison Stickle, bear right to the summit.

Ascent from Stonethwaite 2 *off map N*

The long stride from Rosthwaite (7km) or Stonethwaite (5.5km) up Langstrath to the top of Stake Pass is normally undertaken as part of the Cumbria Way but also offers a straightforward route to the Langdale Pikes from Borrowdale.

Via Langstrath →8.7km/5½ miles ↑640m/2100ft ⏱3hr
3 Follow the lane through the hamlet. The gated track passes above the popular camping meadow, latterly passing Alisongrass Hoghouse camping barn.

As the beck comes closer listen to the roar of Galleny Force down in the tree cover to the left. The track bends right, via a gate, beside the clear cascading waters of **Langstrath Beck**, through a gate to a footbridge.

Follow the west side footpath that climbs over the ladder-stile at Blackmoss, and, at this point, look up to the left for climbers scaling Sergeant's Crag Slabs. Below and above Black Moss Pot the beck takes a wide, shingled, meandering course, with the craggy slopes of Rosthwaite Fall and Glaramara high to the right. (Alternatively cross the beck to take a closer look at Black Moss Pot, a famous swimming haunt, and cross back at Tray Dub footbridge.) At the end of the valley, follow the bridleway up to **Stake Pass**.

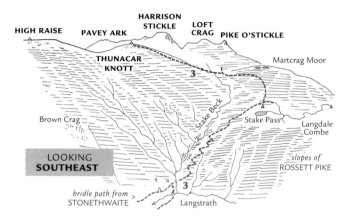

From the cairn at the top of the pass a strong path branches south onto the peaty ridge of **Martcrag Moor**, traversing some pretty horrid ground before the slope steepens. Coming close to a gill, branch half-left (east-southeast) from the main path to Pike o'Stickle. Rising up the grassy fell, skirt the rocky rim to reach the summit cairn.

The summit

There are two tops, each with a cairn, to the north and south of a shallow hollow filled with a pool. The southern cairn is 'the' summit, whatever the quirks of tradition may try to claim – in my book the top of a fell is the summit! The

Pike o'Stickle from the summit outcrop

panorama is the meat of the matter – there is a lot to see, but qualitatively the view is at its best to the west.

Safe descents

A narrow trod leads due S into Harrison Combe and joins the path (**1**) directly below Harrison Crag above the upper Dungeon Ghyll gorge. It runs perilously along the rim of the ravine, so care is needed here. An alternative option would be to cross the large stepping-stones and make for the Thorn Crag col joining Mark Gate, a very well-secured path that leaves from Loft Crag. Both routes reach down to the New Dungeon Ghyll.

Ridge routes

Harrison Stickle →*0.8km/½ mile* ↓*45m/150ft* ↑*60m/200ft* ⏱*20min*
Head S largely over grassy terrain and eventually swerve to the right of a rock tor to reach the summit.

High Raise →*1.6km/1 mile* ↓*50m/160ft* ↑*85m/280ft* ⏱*35min*
At last a chance to lengthen the stride. Go north, drifting down to join the ridge path from Pavey Ark, and cross the depression at the head of Bright Beck. Beyond, the path has been realigned to reduce wear on fragile soil along the gentle rise to the summit.

Sergeant Man →*1.6km/1 mile* ↓*45m/150ft* ↑*60m/200ft* ⏱*30min*
Go N with the High Raise path, only take the second path angling half-right. As the ground begins to rise after the depression contour to the summit knot. (The first path leads through an outcrop and traverses the slope well below Sergeant Man – a kind of speedy short-cut for anyone racing to Grasmere. Shame on them!)

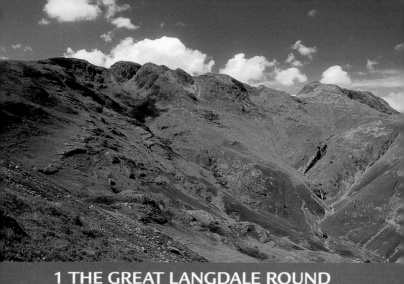

1 THE GREAT LANGDALE ROUND

Start/Finish	Old Dungeon Ghyll **18**
Distance	18km (11 miles)
Ascent/Descent	1530m (5020ft)
Time	9hr
Terrain	Requires good weather as the route does not always follow the main paths. Competence in a challenging mountain environment is a pre-requisite.
Summits	Pike o'Blisco, Crinkle Crags, Bowfell and Rossett Pike

It's hard to think of a more complete and compelling mountain day on the high fells. Strong walkers will be capable of gathering up the Langdale Pikes, too, beyond Stake Pass, but to my mind they are seen at their best from various stations on this circuit.

Follow the road back from the car park and at the bus stop bear right with the road by **Wall End** farm, crossing the cattle grid and winding up the hill. At the third bend a clear path leads off right: this is the main route up the **Redacre Gill** valley. The path is well-marked and, after fording three gills, becomes

↑ *Crinkle Crags and Bowfell from Pike o'Blisco*   219

beautifully pitched rising steeply onto the plateau. It weaves on glancing to the right of a large block slab. As you come to the wedding-cake upper cap of the fell, rock bands and three distinct scramble pitches bring hands and feet into action to reach the gap between the twin summits of **Pike o'Blisco**.

The NW summit has the best view of the walk ahead, while the SW summit displays the Coniston fells. Leave the summit SW on the palpable path descending into the shallow depression N of **Red Tarn**. After the path intersection step over the outflowing gill now on a gradual climb W. The formerly broad and straggly path is now tightened by flanking stones but it can be loose at times. Bypass **Great Knott** on your right, or step off the path to visit this worthy viewpoint.

The path angles NW to reach the first crinkle up a rock-step. Cross over into the grassy gap with its stunning view back down Great Cove towards Oxendale. To avoid a scramble, trend half-left passing below a rock wall to mount onto the western end of **Long Top**. Otherwise tackle the 'Bad Step' head on. From the summit cairn of **Crinkle Crags** descend over characteristically stony ground, no two steps the same!

From here, the main path initially angles NE from the summit cairn passing the top of the deep gully of Mickle Door to cross three rocky crests – or might they be crinkles? The last, known as **Gunson Knott**, provides a fine view into Great Langdale and the Scafells are over to your left, never far out of sight, as you weave a course N, claiming all or some of the tops en route to the **Three Tarns** col.

Three Tarns offers a moment's pause and a possible opportunity to play with reflections of the Scafells in your camera lens and admire the impressive Links crags above the impending scree of Bowfell. A worn trail sets about the steep, loose climb with some critical pitching, swinging NW as you come above Flat Crags, the Great Slab providing a thrilling foreground. The slope eases to reach the cairn surmounting the summit pyramid of **Bowfell**.

Head NNW over the stony summit plateau with cairns guiding to dip into the comparatively shallow pass of **Ore Gap**. Due NW from the pass sits the tempting rocky top of Esk Pike, but it is not integral to the skyline route. Our ridge walk breaks right from the col descending often over rough terrain to join the path from Sty Head, leading down by the outflow of **Angle Tarn**. Stepping over the stones the path forks (the leftward path leading to Stake

Pass). Keep ahead rising to the brow. Side-step left to visit the comparatively low-set summit of **Rossett Pike** – a great place to view the Hanging Knotts of Bowfell and, from the east cairn, the deep valley gulf of Mickleden, with Pike o'Stickle impressive in elegant profile.

Step back to the brow and join the well-engineered path winding down the **Rossett Gill** fellside, thankfully no longer resorting to the shocking depths of the gill itself, the long descent completed at a large ragged cairn directing walkers to Esk Hause and Stake Pass. Cross the wooden bridge parallel with the drumlin field over to the right and trace the flat-bottomed dale floor of

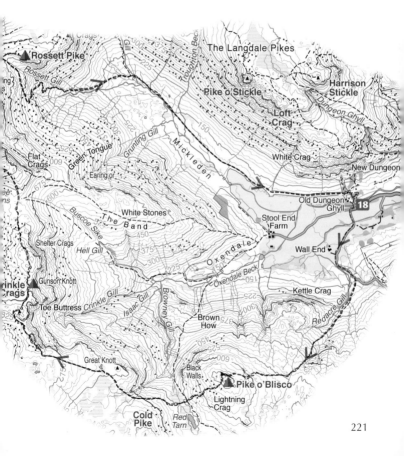

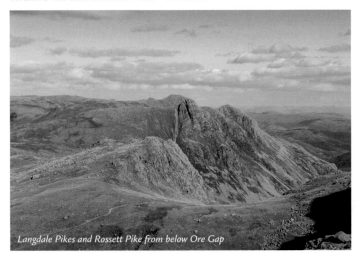

Langdale Pikes and Rossett Pike from below Ore Gap

Mickleden, with more impressive views upwards to Pike o'Stickle and Gimmer Crag. Soon after the track is joined by a wall from the right which takes you through successive gates. After the final gate the track brings you triumphantly in behind the **Old Dungeon Ghyll** hotel to conclude a memorable day.

2 THE LANGDALE PIKES

Start/Finish	Stickle Ghyll **17**
Distance	10.5km (6½ miles)
Ascent/Descent	945m (3100ft)
Time	5hr
Terrain	Largely on good, clear paths, but the descent from the ridge SE of Sergeant Man is not obvious, the path sporadic early on through craggy terrain.
Summits	Loft Crag, Pike o'Stickle, Harrison Stickle, Thunacar Knott, High Raise and Sergeant Man

A walk of wonderful contrasts. The secure climb up Mark Gate gives access to three summits flanking Harrison Combe, only Pike o'Stickle offering real rocky resistance. The journey north over Thunacar Knott to High Raise and back southeast by Sergeant Man encourages a free-flowing stride. Lower down in the shy valley east of Tarn Crag the green track is a seldom-savoured joy.

Leave the car park behind Sticklebarn by a hand-gate and pass through a walled passage onto a pitched path. After the National Trust marker stone the path forks. Bear left with the loose stony trail, rising to a kissing-gate. Keep up

right, beside the rising wall, to a tall stile, after which carefully ford **Dungeon Ghyll** to climb with Mark Gate, an old shepherding way. Keep a watch for the particularly fine view of the mare's-tail falls in the ravine to the right. The stepped path reaches the ridge comfortably between Thorn Crag and Loft Crag. Keeping left soon find a loose stony path slanting up left to gain the top of **Loft Crag**.

Pass over by the cairn following the ridge, lured on by the superb dome of Pike o'Stickle. As you arrive above the deep gully of South Screes use the

steps and then scramble to the very topmost cairn. **Pike o'Stickle** is an exceptional crest, fashioned from a volcano vent, making it extra resistant to glacial erosion. Retrace your clambering ascent and cut right to cross Harrison Combe on a cairned path, with stepping-stones over the principal draining gill. One short rock scramble and the way to the broad rock top of **Harrison Stickle** is assured.

Depart NNW keeping to the spine of the ridge with minor rocks and pools to divert you before the next rise onto **Thunacar Knott**, the cairn set in splintered bedrock. The palpable path declines into the shallow dip in the broad grassy ridge where it forks. Resist the temptation to curve gently right to Sergeant Man direct and forge on a little further to **High White Stones** and the great wind-shelter and OS column on **High Raise**. This is an inspiring spot with the best of the view to the west and north.

Turn back SE passing the N shore of the plateau tarn, with an abundance of peat and pools as you draw closer to **Sergeant Man**. Clamber easily onto the bare rock top with its modest cairn overlooking the wild Bright Beck valley-head. Step back down and follow the clear path which angles SE after passing the big rock slab and curving under a low dark rock-face. Look out for a cairn where the path to Easedale Tarn breaks left at a right-angle. Ignore this to continue forward for 200m and then fork half-right. Three cairns give a clue to the way off the ridge S. The path is spasmodic at best, threading down grassy banks between large outcrops and for a short while accompanying a gill, but it soon veers left. After a small walled enclosure under a rock wall the path becomes more defined.

Do not be lured towards **Stickle Tarn**, loomed over by the stupendous craggy face of Pavey Ark. When you come to a sharp bend right in that direction, go straight on (S) to find a lovely zig-zagging green path. This comes down beside a large upland walled enclosure in a shy side valley and passes a roofless shepherd's bothy, now with the looming presence of Tarn Crag up to the right. Eventually, the path comes closer to the tumbling beck to join the popular pitched path descending from the shores of Stickle Tarn. Go left naturally following this stepped way zig-zagging down to join a second pitched way, continuing with the excitement of Stickle Ghyll's dancing cascades ever present nearby. As you reach a stand of conifers, cross the tall stile to complete your descent.

Herdwick ewes being driven between pastures

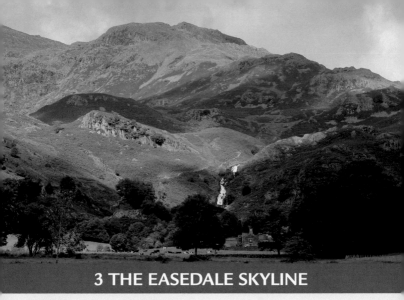

3 THE EASEDALE SKYLINE

Start/Finish	Red Bank Road **8**
Distance	14km (8¾ miles)
Ascent/Descent	735m (2410ft)
Time	6hr
Terrain	In mist this route can be tricky. From Tarn Crag to Sergeant Man there is little hint of a consistent path. For all its popularity, neither is the oft boggy and rocky knolled ridge by Blea Rigg a straightforward way.
Summits	Tarn Crag, Sergeant Man, Blea Rigg and Silver How

A rousing walk best tackled anti-clockwise for the growing sense of excitement leading up to Sergeant Man where the Langdale Pikes burst upon the scene. From this point you can feast your eyes on close-up and far-off mountain scenery, with the enticing view down into the Vale of Grasmere from Silver How a final flourish to relish.

From the car park follow Langdale Road by Tweedies into Broadgate to reach Sam Read's Bookshop. Turn left onto Easedale Road. After Goody Bridge, as

↑ *Your first objective, Tarn Crag, from Easedale*

Blea Rigg from Sergeant Man

Easedale Beck flows close to the road, get your first clear view of Tarn Crag and Sour Milk Gill. The road opens through a meadow by Parrock Lodge coming to the private road for Brimmer Head farm. Turn an abrupt right, signed for Far Easedale. A confined path, rough underfoot then cobbled, leads up by a gate. Bear left and keep within the lower walled lane. This opens and runs on beside a wall, rising to come by a large glacial slab, now beside **Far Easedale Gill**. A little further on, arrive at the wooden **Stythwaite Steps** footbridge.

Cross the bridge and follow on with the footpath (leaving the valley-floor path). Keep up left in near proximity to the wall through bracken. The wall ghosts away left before you come over the brow which offers a view into a broad hollow. Branch from the regular trail onto a minor trod climbing up right through the bracken with the natural pull of the ridge drawing you ever more insistently. Happily grass takes over on the rocky ridge. Easedale Tarn captures your attention down to the left in the hanging valley set well below the dark wall of Blea Crag. Head purposefully to the definite peak ahead with the fierce precipice of **Deer Bield Crag** down to the right. Ultimately round the neat rocky head on the right hand side, setting foot on the fine perch of **Tarn Crag** beside the cairn.

228

The ridge west is quite broad though irregular, with a path to match, evading bogs and rocky knolls, becoming ever more vague. The ground steepens, with no hint of a path, gaining a fine view down on an upper hollow cradling Codale Tarn. This is fellwandering pure and simple. Climb over the brow at a prominent rocky top to join a path rising from Broadstone Head, which follows the line of metal stakes (lost fence) to the castle-like crest of **Codale Head**.

Spurning High Raise only 2km away, keep to the spirit of the circuit and descend W and curve SW round the pool-bejewelled hollow to climb the eminent knob of **Sergeant Man**. This unsung summit deserves more recognition and is the skyline climax and key turning-point of your horseshoe.

The journey now turns to the eastward ridge running SE, an unfailing delight from start to its finish upon Silver How. Descend on a clear path faithful to the ridge. Passing a great bare slab and a tiny rock-girt pool, with Pavey Ark and Harrison Stickle now seen to perfection, frequent backward glances

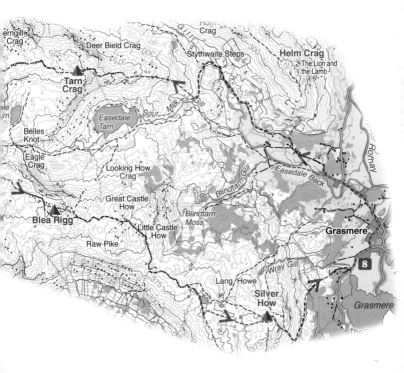

draw the eye back to Sergeant Man before attention turns to the rock crest of **Blea Rigg**. Follow the leftward path but step off to the right to claim the summit and just step back to weave on through a splendid landscape of splintered rock crests and moorland bog, dotted with a variety of pools. In fine weather this is a walkers' paradise but in mist the lattice of paths can be confusing.

The character of the ridge gradually changes after **Raw Pike**. Grassy banks take over and, a large cairn passed, soon the abrupt headland of **Lang Howe** catches attention to the left above a vegetated pool as the summit cairn of **Silver How** is finally reached. Stop and take in the sylvan Vale of Grasmere.

Descend N and quickly, sharp right, soon aided by pitched steps down the stony defile. As the slopes ease the pitching is lost in the bracken as you reach a wall. Turn left descending with the well-built wall close at hand by three kissing-gates, latterly within a walled lane, to a gate onto the road opposite Faeryland tea garden and boat hire. Turn left to walk down and complete the circuit.

Great slab beside the path near Stythwaite Steps

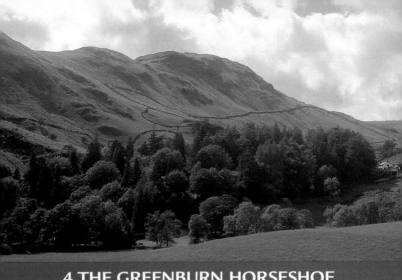

4 THE GREENBURN HORSESHOE

Start/Finish	Red Bank Road **8**
Distance	12km (7½ miles)
Ascent/Descent	780m (2560ft)
Time	5hr
Terrain	Marshy ground during the first half of the connection from Calf Crag to Steel Fell is the one navigational hazard in mist.
Summits	Helm Crag, Gibson Knott, Calf Crag and Steel Fell

The natural skyline of the shy Greenburn valley comprises a quartet of summits. Many walkers simply clamber up and straight down Helm Crag, but this does not do this ridge-end height justice as it is by rights far more impressively seen in the context of this round trip.

From the car park follow Langdale Road by Tweedies into Broadgate to reach Sam Read's Bookshop. Turn left here up Easedale Road. A little way along an off-road path is available on the left of the road. Soon after Goody Bridge, spanning **Easedale Beck**, the road opens through a meadow by Parrock Lodge

⬆ *The northern end of Helm Crag and Gibson Knott from Town Head*

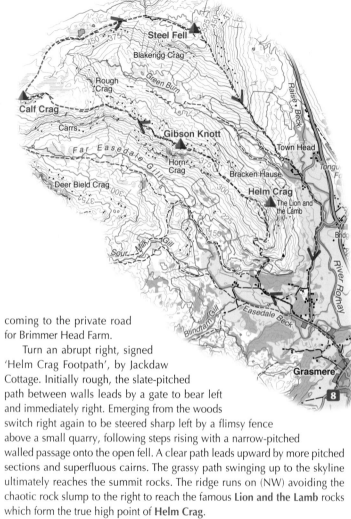

coming to the private road
for Brimmer Head Farm.

Turn an abrupt right, signed
'Helm Crag Footpath', by Jackdaw
Cottage. Initially rough, the slate-pitched
path between walls leads by a gate to bear left
and immediately right. Emerging from the woods
switch right again to be steered sharp left by a flimsy fence
above a small quarry, following steps rising with a narrow-pitched
walled passage onto the open fell. A clear path leads upward by more pitched
sections and superfluous cairns. The grassy path swinging up to the skyline
ultimately reaches the summit rocks. The ridge runs on (NW) avoiding the
chaotic rock slump to the right to reach the famous **Lion and the Lamb** rocks
which form the true high point of **Helm Crag**.

Leave the rocks and head down the bank NW to begin one of the most
pleasing ridge wanders in the district, beyond Bracken Hause seldom con-
sciously on the ridge-top, weaving along on a slender path always favouring
the west side of the ridge until it finally alights upon the summit cairn of

The Howitzer – Helm Crag's summit outcrop (photo: Andrew Leaney)

Gibson Knott. The wilds of Far Easedale lie below and the steep shadowed cliff of Deer Bield Crag with its crazy boulders makes another striking feature of the scene. Over Pike of Carrs next, and then the path finally reaches the cairn marking the top of **Calf Crag**. This is the pivotal point on the round.

Swing N then NE to find a path that leads by modest ridged ground toward the twin pools on the flat ridge. From here the fragmentary stakes of an old metal fence lead irresistibly E. As the ridge rises the fence is intact, mounting to the reddish-stoned summit cairn marking **Steel Fell**, otherwise known as Dead Pike. A small cairn with a metal stake set into a rock lures you further E on from the fence to enjoy the view over Dunmail Raise. Turn SE following the oft steep switchback path down to the grassy ridge and via a kissing-gate and then successive field gates through the lower enclosures to meet the tarmac road at Turn Howe, coming down by Helmside to cross **Green Burn** by its confluence with **Raise Beck**. Keep right at Low Mill Bridge heading for Goody Bridge to reconnect with the Easedale Road and turn left back into the village.

MORE TO EXPLORE

Circular

- from Stickle Ghyll **17**: Pike o'Blisco–Crinkle Crags–Bowfell–Rossett Pike–Pike o'Stickle–Harrison Stickle–Blea Rigg

Linear

- Ambleside **12** to Stickle Ghyll **17**: Loughrigg Fell–Silver How–Blea Rigg
- Old Dungeon Ghyll **18** to Wasdale Head **27**: Bowfell–Esk Pike–Great End–Scafell Pike

The Langdale Pikes from Great Knott

Tourist information

There are no national park information centres in the area covered by this guide but lots of information is available on the national park website: www.lakedistrict. gov.uk.

If you want to talk to someone about what you need, the closest centres are in Bowness (National Park) and Ambleside.

Bowness-on-Windermere

0845 901 0845

(calls cost 2p per minute on top of your phone company's access charge)

BownessTIC@lakedistrict.gov.uk

Ambleside

0844 225 0544

tic@thehubofambleside.com

Accommodation

In addition to the tourist information centres, and the search engines, the Visit Cumbria website has a good database of local accommodation options: www.visitcumbria.com.

Weather

It is well worth consulting either of these forecasts to gauge the best times to be on the tops.

Lake District Weatherline

0844 846 2444

www.lakedistrictweatherline.co.uk

Mountain Weather Information Service

Fully daily mountain forecasts for 3 days at a time (choose Lake District)

www.mwis.org.uk

(choose English and Welsh Forecast/ Lake District)

App: Mountain Forecast Viewer

Transport
Traveline

Bus, train and coach information

www.traveline.info

Stagecoach

Bus information

www.stagecoachbus.com

App: Stagecoach Bus

Organisations
The National Trust

The National Trust owns 90% of the farms in the national park, as well as historic sites and properties, camp sites and car parks.

www.nationaltrust.org.uk

App: National Trust – Days Out

Fix the Fells

Fix the Fells repairs and maintains 330 upland paths in the national park. Read about their work, volunteer or donate on this website.

www.fixthefells.co.uk

Mountain Rescue

The Lake District Search and Mountain Rescue Association manages 12 teams of volunteers across the national park. The site has useful safety information. Downloading the free OS Locate app will enable you to tell the team your grid ref, whether you have phone signal or not, should you need to call them.

www.ldsamra.org.uk

A FELLRANGER'S GLOSSARY

Navigational features

word	explanation
arête	knife-edge ridge
band	binding strip of land
beck	main stream flowing into and through valleys to lakes and rivers
boiler-plates	non-technical term for exposed broad slabs of rock
cairn/man	small pile of loose stones indicating a path or path junction
comb/cove	hanging valley high in the fells
common	undivided land grazed by several farmers
crag	substantial outcrop of rock
dale	valley
dodd	rounded hilltop
drumlin	large mound accumulated beneath a melting glacier
dub	dark pool
fell	mountain pasture, frequently attributed to the whole hill
force	waterfall
garth	small enclosure close to farm-buildings
gate	dialect term for a track
ghyll/gill	steeply sloping watercourse
glen	from British term 'glyn', meaning valley
grain	lesser watercourse above confluence
hag	eroded section of peat-moor
hause, saddle, col, dore, scarth	high gap between fells
holm	dry riverside meadow
hope	secluded valley
howe	hill or mound
ill treacherous	
in-bye pastures	enclosed valley pastures below the rough common grazing
intake	upper limit of valley enclosure
keld	spring
knott	compact or rugged hilltop
ling	heather

lonnin	quiet lane
mell	bald hill
mere	pool or lake
mire	marshy ground
moraine	residual valley-head pillow mound debris left once a glacier melts away
nab	hill-spur or nose
ness	promontory
nether	lower
nook	secluded corner
outcrop	crag or obvious collection of rocks
raise	heap of stones
rake	grooved track
ridding	(the action of) clearing
rigg	ridge
park	enclosed hunting ground
pike	sharp or rocky summit
re-entrant	small valley on the side of a fell where water often collects and is funnelled down the hill (seen as a small V or U shape in a contour line on the map)
place	plot of ground
scale	summer pasture shieling (hut)
scarp/scar	steep hillside
scree	weathered rock debris beneath a crag
seat	summer pasture/high place
shaw	small wood
shelter-cairn	circular windbreak wall
sike	small stream
slack	small, shallow or stony valley
slump	sedimentary rock that has slipped creating dykes (intrusions), fractures or ridges
stang	pole
stead	site of farm
sty	steep path
swine	pigs

tarn	small mountain pool from the Norse 'tjorn', meaning tear
traverse	walking route across the fells
trod	path created by animals
trig point	Ordnance Survey triangulation column
thwaite	clearing
wick	inlet or bay or subsidiary farm
water	feeder lake to river
wath	ford
whin	gorse
wray	secluded corner
yeat	gate

Place names

name	**explanation**
Angle Tarn	tarn stocked with fish by miners to supplement their diet by angling
Blind (Tarn)	with a hidden outflow
Codale Head	cold dalehead
Copt Howe	look-out hillock
Earing Crag	= eyrie crag, nesting site for an eagle
Easedale	from the personal name Asi (Norse), first mentioned in 1332
Gimmer (Crag)	gimmer = ewe-lamb between its first and second shearing
Goody Bridge	from the personal name Guddy, recorded in 1586
Kettle Crag	with a spring that issues like boiling water
Martcrag Moor	mart = pine marten
Lanty Scar	from the personal name Lancelot
Little Parrock	little paddock
Pianet Knott	magpie's rocks
Stythwaite (Steps)	steep clearing
Three Shire Stone	A stone which, prior to 1974, marked the meeting point of Cumberland, Westmorland and Lancashire. (The current stone is a replacement which only names Lancashire.)

Throstle Garth	from the personal name Frostildr (Norse) + deer fence
Turn Howe	thorn mound
Ullet Nest (Cottage)	owl's nest
Whorneyside	wren's fell pasture
Wrynose Pass	stallion pass (requiring extra horsepower!)
Yeastyrigg Crags	ridge that rises (as if it had yeast in it)

Fell names

Just the more intriguing ones...

name	explanation
Blea Rigg	bleak ridge
Bowfell	bowed mountain
Calf Crag	subsidiary outlying summit
Cold Pike	exposed peak
Gibson Knott	rocky summit belonging to Gibson
Harrison Stickle	pointed peak associated with the Harrison family
Lingmoor Fell	heather-clad hill
Loughrigg Fell	ridge above a lake (Loughrigg Tarn)
Pavey Ark	Peak above Pavia's summer shieling
Rossett Pike	peak of the high pastures where the horses were kept
Sergeant Man	boundary cairn (of Egremont) set by the land-sergeant
Tarn Crag	rocky peak above a lake (Easedale Tarn)
Thunacar Knott	rocks threaded by long wavy grasses

THE LAKE DISTRICT FELLS

Fell name	Height	Volume
Allen Crags	784m/2572ft	Borrowdale
Angletarn Pikes	567m/1860ft	Mardale and the Far East
Ard Crags	581m/1906ft	Buttermere
Armboth Fell	479m/1572ft	Borrowdale
Arnison Crag	434m/1424ft	Patterdale
Arthur's Pike	533m/1749ft	Mardale and the Far East
Bakestall	673m/2208ft	Keswick and the North
Bannerdale Crags	683m/2241ft	Keswick and the North
Barf	468m/1535ft	Keswick and the North
Barrow	456m/1496ft	Buttermere
Base Brown	646m/2119ft	Borrowdale
Beda Fell	509m/1670ft	Mardale and the Far East
Bell Crags	558m/1831ft	Borrowdale
Binsey	447m/1467ft	Keswick and the North
Birkhouse Moor	718m/2356ft	Patterdale
Birks	622m/2241ft	Patterdale
Black Combe	600m/1969ft	Coniston
Black Fell	323m/1060ft	Coniston
Blake Fell	573m/1880ft	Buttermere
Bleaberry Fell	589m/1932ft	Borrowdale
Blea Rigg	556m/1824ft	Langdale
Blencathra	868m/2848ft	Keswick and the North
Bonscale Pike	529m/1736ft	Mardale and the Far East
Bowfell	903m/2963ft	Langdale
Bowscale Fell	702m/2303ft	Keswick and the North
Brae Fell	586m/1923ft	Keswick and the North
Brandreth	715m/2346ft	Borrowdale
Branstree	713m/2339ft	Mardale and the Far East
Brim Fell	795m/2608ft	Coniston

Fell name	Height	Volume
Brock Crags	561m/1841ft	Mardale and the Far East
Broom Fell	511m/1676ft	Keswick and the North
Buckbarrow (Corney Fell)	549m/1801ft	Coniston
Buckbarrow (Wast Water)	430m/1411ft	Wasdale
Calf Crag	537m/1762ft	Langdale
Carl Side	746m/2448ft	Keswick and the North
Carrock Fell	662m/2172ft	Keswick and the North
Castle Crag	290m/951ft	Borrowdale
Catbells	451m/1480ft	Borrowdale
Catstycam	890m/2920ft	Patterdale
Caudale Moor	764m/2507ft	Mardale and the Far East
Causey Pike	637m/2090ft	Buttermere
Caw	529m/1736ft	Coniston
Caw Fell	697m/2287ft	Wasdale
Clough Head	726m/2386ft	Patterdale
Cold Pike	701m/2300ft	Langdale
Coniston Old Man	803m/2635ft	Coniston
Crag Fell	523m/1716ft	Wasdale
Crag Hill	839m/2753ft	Buttermere
Crinkle Crags	840m/2756ft	Langdale
Dale Head	753m/2470ft	Buttermere
Dodd	502m/1647ft	Keswick and the North
Dollywaggon Pike	858m/2815ft	Patterdale
Dove Crag	792m/2599ft	Patterdale
Dow Crag	778m/2553ft	Coniston
Eagle Crag	520m/1706ft	Borrowdale
Eskdale Moor	337m/1105ft	Wasdale
Esk Pike	885m/2904ft	Langdale
Fairfield	873m/2864ft	Patterdale

Fell name	Height	Volume
Fellbarrow	416m/1365ft	Buttermere
Fleetwith Pike	648m/2126ft	Buttermere
Froswick	720m/2362ft	Mardale and the Far East
Gavel Fell	526m/1726ft	Buttermere
Gibson Knott	421m/1381ft	Langdale
Glaramara	783m/2569ft	Borrowdale
Glenridding Dodd	442m/1450ft	Patterdale
Gowbarrow Fell	481m/1578ft	Patterdale
Grange Fell	416m/1365ft	Borrowdale
Grasmoor	852m/2795ft	Buttermere
Gray Crag	697m/2287ft	Mardale and the Far East
Grayrigg Forest	494m/1621ft	Mardale and the Far East
Graystones	456m/1496ft	Keswick and the North
Great Borne	616m/2021ft	Buttermere
Great Calva	690m/2264ft	Keswick and the North
Great Carrs	788m/2585ft	Coniston
Great Cockup	526m/1726ft	Keswick and the North
Great Crag	452m/1483ft	Borrowdale
Great Dodd	857m/2812ft	Patterdale
Great End	907m/2976ft	Borrowdale, Langdale, Wasdale
Great Gable	899m/2949ft	Borrowdale, Wasdale
Great How	523m/1716ft	Wasdale
Great Mell Fell	537m/1762ft	Patterdale
Great Rigg	767m/2516ft	Patterdale
Great Sca Fell	651m/2136ft	Keswick and the North
Great Worm Crag	427m/1401ft	Coniston
Green Crag	489m/1604ft	Coniston
Green Gable	801m/2628ft	Borrowdale
Grey Crag	638m/2093ft	Mardale and the Far East

Fell name	Height	Volume
Grey Friar	772m/2533ft	Coniston
Grey Knotts	697m/2287ft	Borrowdale
Grike	488m/1601ft	Wasdale
Grisedale Pike	791m/2595ft	Buttermere
Hallin Fell	388m/1273ft	Mardale and the Far East
Hard Knott	552m/1811ft	Coniston
Harrison Stickle	736m/2415ft	Langdale
Hart Crag	822m/2697ft	Patterdale
Harter Fell (Eskdale)	653m/2142ft	Coniston
Harter Fell (Mardale and the Far East)	778m/2553ft	Mardale and the Far East
Hart Side	758m/2487ft	Patterdale
Hartsop above How	586m/1923ft	Patterdale
Hartsop Dodd	618m/2028ft	Mardale and the Far East
Haycock	798m/2618ft	Wasdale
Haystacks	598m/1962ft	Buttermere
Helm Crag	405m/1329ft	Langdale
Helvellyn	950m/3116ft	Patterdale
Hen Comb	509m/1670ft	Buttermere
Heron Pike	621m/2037ft	Patterdale
Hesk Fell	476m/1562ft	Coniston
High Crag	744m/2441ft	Buttermere
High Hartsop Dodd	519m/1703ft	Patterdale
High Pike (Caldbeck)	658m/2159ft	Keswick and the North
High Pike (Scandale Fell)	656m/2152ft	Patterdale
High Raise (Central Fells)	762m/2500ft	Langdale
High Raise (Haweswater)	802m/2631ft	Mardale and the Far East
High Rigg	355m/1165ft	Borrowdale
High Seat	608m/1995ft	Borrowdale
High Spy	653m/2142ft	Borrowdale

Fell name	Height	Volume
High Stile	807m/2648ft	Buttermere
High Street	828m/2717ft	Mardale and the Far East
High Tove	515m/1690ft	Borrowdale
Hindscarth	727m/2385ft	Buttermere
Holme Fell	317m/1040ft	Coniston
Hopegill Head	770m/2526ft	Buttermere
Ill Bell	757m/2484ft	Mardale and the Far East
Illgill Head	609m/1998ft	Wasdale
Iron Crag	640m/2100ft	Wasdale
Kentmere Pike	730m/2395ft	Mardale and the Far East
Kidsty Pike	780m/2559ft	Mardale and the Far East
Kirk Fell	802m/2631ft	Wasdale
Knock Murton	447m/1467ft	Buttermere
Knott	710m/2329ft	Keswick and the North
Knott Rigg	556m/1824ft	Buttermere
Lank Rigg	541m/1775ft	Wasdale
Latrigg	368m/1207ft	Keswick and the North
Ling Fell	373m/1224ft	Keswick and the North
Lingmell	807m/2649ft	Wasdale
Lingmoor Fell	470m/1542ft	Langdale
Little Hart Crag	637m/2090ft	Patterdale
Little Mell Fell	505m/1657ft	Patterdale
Little Stand	739m/2426ft	Langdale
Loadpot Hill	671m/2201ft	Mardale and the Far East
Loft Crag	682m/2237ft	Langdale
Longlands Fell	483m/1585ft	Keswick and the North
Long Side	734m/2408ft	Keswick and the North
Lonscale Fell	715m/2346ft	Keswick and the North
Lord's Seat	552m/1811ft	Keswick and the North

Fell name	Height	Volume
Loughrigg Fell	335m/1099ft	Langdale
Low Fell	423m/1388ft	Buttermere
Low Pike	507m/1663ft	Patterdale
Maiden Moor	576m/1890ft	Borrowdale
Mardale Ill Bell	761m/2497ft	Mardale and the Far East
Meal Fell	550m/1804ft	Keswick and the North
Mellbreak	512m/1680ft	Buttermere
Middle Dodd	653m/2143ft	Patterdale
Middle Fell	585m/1919ft	Wasdale
Muncaster Fell	231m/758ft	Coniston
Nab Scar	450m/1476ft	Patterdale
Nethermost Pike	891m/2923ft	Patterdale
Outerside	568m/1863ft	Buttermere
Pavey Ark	697m/2287ft	Langdale
Pike o'Blisco	705m/2313ft	Langdale
Pike o'Stickle	708m/2323ft	Langdale
Pillar	892m/2926ft	Wasdale
Place Fell	657m/2155ft	Mardale and the Far East
Raise	884m/2900ft	Patterdale
Rampsgill Head	792m/2598ft	Mardale and the Far East
Rannerdale Knotts	355m/1165ft	Buttermere
Raven Crag	463m/1519ft	Borrowdale
Red Pike (Buttermere)	755m/2477ft	Buttermere
Red Pike (Wasdale)	828m/2717ft	Wasdale
Red Screes	777m/2549ft	Patterdale
Rest Dodd	697m/2287ft	Mardale and the Far East
Robinson	737m/2418ft	Buttermere
Rossett Pike	651m/2136ft	Langdale
Rosthwaite Fell	551m/1808ft	Borrowdale

Fell name	Height	Volume
Sail	771m/2529ft	Buttermere
Sale Fell	359m/1178ft	Keswick and the North
Sallows	516m/1693ft	Mardale and the Far East
Scafell	964m/3163ft	Wasdale
Scafell Pike	977m/3206ft	Borrowdale, Langdale, Wasdale
Scar Crags	672m/2205ft	Buttermere
Scoat Fell	843m/2766ft	Wasdale
Seatallan	693m/2274ft	Wasdale
Seathwaite Fell	631m/2070ft	Borrowdale
Seat Sandal	736m/2415ft	Patterdale
Selside Pike	655m/2149ft	Mardale and the Far East
Sergeant Man	736m/2414ft	Langdale
Sergeant's Crag	574m/1883ft	Borrowdale
Sheffield Pike	675m/2215ft	Patterdale
Shipman Knotts	587m/1926ft	Mardale and the Far East
Silver How	395m/1296ft	Langdale
Skiddaw	931m/3054ft	Keswick and the North
Skiddaw Little Man	865m/2838ft	Keswick and the North
Slight Side	762m/2500ft	Wasdale
Souther Fell	522m/1713ft	Keswick and the North
Stainton Pike	498m/1634ft	Coniston
Starling Dodd	635m/2083ft	Buttermere
Steel Fell	553m/1814ft	Langdale
Steel Knotts	433m/1421ft	Mardale and the Far East
Steeple	819m/2687ft	Wasdale
Stickle Pike	376m/1234ft	Coniston
Stone Arthur	503m/1650ft	Patterdale
St Sunday Crag	841m/2759ft	Patterdale

Fell name	Height	Volume
Stybarrow Dodd	846m/2776ft	Patterdale
Swirl How	804m/2638ft	Coniston
Tarn Crag (Easedale)	485m/1591ft	Langdale
Tarn Crag (Longsleddale)	664m/2179ft	Mardale and the Far East
Thornthwaite Crag	784m/2572ft	Mardale and the Far East
Thunacar Knott	723m/2372ft	Langdale
Troutbeck Tongue	363m/1191ft	Mardale and the Far East
Ullock Pike	690m/2264ft	Keswick and the North
Ullscarf	726m/2382ft	Borrowdale
Walla Crag	379m/1243ft	Borrowdale
Wallowbarrow Crag	292m/958ft	Coniston
Walna Scar	621m/2037ft	Coniston
Wandope	772m/2533ft	Buttermere
Wansfell	489m/1604ft	Mardale and the Far East
Watson's Dodd	789m/2589ft	Patterdale
Wether Hill	673m/2208ft	Mardale and the Far East
Wetherlam	762m/2500ft	Coniston
Whinfell Beacon	494m/1620ft	Mardale and the Far East
Whinlatter	517m/1696ft	Keswick and the North
Whin Rigg	536m/1759ft	Wasdale
Whiteless Pike	660m/2165ft	Buttermere
Whiteside	707m/2320ft	Buttermere
White Side	863m/2831ft	Patterdale
Whitfell	573m/1880ft	Coniston
Winterscleugh	471m/1545ft	Mardale and the Far East
Yewbarrow	628m/2060ft	Wasdale
Yoadcastle	494m/1621ft	Coniston
Yoke	706m/2316ft	Mardale and the Far East

Walking – Trekking – Mountaineering – Climbing – Cycling

Over 50 years, Cicerone have built up an outstanding collection of over 300 guides, inspiring all sorts of amazing adventures.

Every guide comes from extensive exploration and research by our expert authors, all with a passion for their subjects. They are frequently praised, endorsed and used by clubs, instructors and outdoor organisations.

All our titles can now be bought as **e-books**, **ePubs** and **Kindle** files and we also have an online magazine – **Cicerone Extra** – with features to help cyclists, climbers, walkers and trekkers choose their next adventure, at home or abroad.

Our website shows any **new information** we've had in since a book was published. Please do let us know if you find anything has changed, so that we can publish the latest details. On our **website** you'll also find great ideas and lots of detailed information about what's inside every guide and you can buy **individual routes** from many of them online.

It's easy to keep in touch with what's going on at Cicerone by getting our monthly **free e-newsletter**, which is full of offers, competitions, up-to-date information and topical articles. You can subscribe on our home page and also follow us on **Facebook** and **Twitter** or dip into our **blog**.

Cicerone – the very best guides for exploring the world.

CICERONE

Juniper House, Murley Moss, Oxenholme Road, Kendal, Cumbria LA9 7RL
Tel: 015395 62069 info@cicerone.co.uk
www.cicerone.co.uk